NEW APPROACHES TO MERGERS AND ACQUISITIONS

THE NEW BUSINESS CULTURE SERIES

Already published

- New Approaches to Recruitment and Selection
- New Approaches to Flexible Working
- New Approaches to Creating a Culture of Innovation

Forthcoming in the series

- New Approaches to the Digitalisation of the Organization
- New Approaches to the Management of Change
- New Approaches to Leadership

NEW APPROACHES TO MERGERS AND ACQUISITIONS

BY

FONS TROMPENAARS
Trompenaars Hampden-Turner Consulting, The Netherlands

and

PETER WOOLLIAMS
Anglia Ruskin, Cambridge, UK

United Kingdom – North America – Japan – India
Malaysia – China

Emerald Publishing Limited
Emerald Publishing, Floor 5, Northspring, 21-23 Wellington Street, Leeds LS1 4DL.

First edition 2025

Copyright © 2025 Fons Trompenaars and Peter Woolliams.
Published under exclusive licence by Emerald Publishing Limited.

Reprints and permissions service
Contact: www.copyright.com

No part of this book may be reproduced, stored in a retrieval system, transmitted in any form or by any means electronic, mechanical, photocopying, recording or otherwise without either the prior written permission of the publisher or a licence permitting restricted copying issued in the UK by The Copyright Licensing Agency and in the USA by The Copyright Clearance Center. No responsibility is accepted for the accuracy of information contained in the text, illustrations or advertisements. The opinions expressed in these chapters are not necessarily those of the Author or the publisher.

British Library Cataloguing in Publication Data
A catalogue record for this book is available from the British Library

ISBN: 978-1-83708-829-4 (Print)
ISBN: 978-1-83708-826-3 (Online)
ISBN: 978-1-83708-828-7 (Epub)

INVESTOR IN PEOPLE

CONTENTS

List of Figures and Tables — ix
About the Authors — xi
Rationale for the Series — xiii
Acknowledgements — xv

1 The Life Curve Is Here to Stay — 1
2 Times of Crisis — 7
3 Reasons Why M&A Programmes Fail to Deliver the Anticipated Benefits — 15
   3.1. Cultural Clash — 15
   3.2. Overestimation of Synergies — 15
   3.3. Integration Difficulties — 16
   3.4. High Costs — 16
   3.5. Inadequate Due Diligence — 16
   3.6. Distraction from Day-to-Day Core Business — 16
   3.7. Lack of Clear Vision and Leadership — 16
   3.8. Market and Economic Conditions — 17
   3.9. Regulatory Hurdles — 17
   3.10. Loss of Key Talent — 17
   3.11. Communication Issues — 17
   3.12. Concluding Comment — 18

4	Context	19
	4.1. The Drive	19
	4.2. It's Not Easy …	20
	4.3. Definitions	21
	4.4. Optimism But Still Failure	22
5	The Hard and Soft Issues	27
	5.1. Failure to Elicit and Focus on the Key Issues	27
	5.1.1. Synergy and Savings Evaluation	27
	5.1.2. Integration Project Planning	28
	5.1.3. Due Diligence	28
	5.2. Failure to Question (Cultural) Assumptions	28
	5.2.1. Selecting the Management Team	29
	5.2.2. Resolving Cultural Issues	29
	5.3. Failure to Communicate Effectively	30
	5.4. Interim Conclusions Concerning M&A Failures	31
	5.5. Merger Goals	32
6	Integrated Value	35
	6.1. Benefits Beyond Shareholder Value	35
	6.2. The Need for a New Systemic and Methodological Framework of Integration	36
7	Our Three Phase Framework	37
	7.1. Step by Step in Three Phases	37
	7.1.1. Phase A: Creating the (Compelling) Business Case	38
	7.1.2. Phase B: Developing Implementation Strategy, Its Objectives, and Key Performance Indicators	39
	7.1.3. Phase C: Developing Systemic Alignment and Value Awareness	39

8 Phase A: Steps Explained 41

- 8.1. Step A1: Redefining Vision and Mission — 41
- 8.2. Step A2: Business Challenges Assessment Through Capturing Business Dilemmas and Their Reconciliation — 44
  - 8.2.1. Our Recompilation Process: Reconciliation of Business Dilemmas or Assessing Integration Potential — 48
  - 8.2.2. The Meta Dilemma of M&As — 53
- 8.3. Step A3: Purpose and Values assessment — 56
  - 8.3.1. Finding Purpose — 56
  - 8.3.2. Approaches to Discovering the Key Purpose — 57
  - 8.3.3. Culture and Values — 57
  - 8.3.4. Why an M&A Software Diagnostic Scan? — 59
  - 8.3.5. Tensions Revealed by Our OCP — 61
  - 8.3.6. Realizing the Business Benefits of the Merger/Acquisition — 65
- 8.4. Step A4: Selecting Values and Effective Behaviours — 66
  - 8.4.1. The Value of Core Values — 67
  - 8.4.2. Conceiving Values as Integral Verbs — 69
  - 8.4.3. Values as Giving Life to Purpose and Mission — 75
  - 8.4.4. Values as Extensions of Personal Values — 75
  - 8.4.5. Exploring the Core Values of the Organisation by Metaphors — 77
  - 8.4.6. The organisation of Core Values — 80
  - 8.4.7. Translating Values into (Effective) Behaviours — 81
  - 8.4.8. Translating V2B: The Integrity Charter — 81
  - 8.4.9. Intact Teams — 84
- 8.5. Step A5: (Revisiting) the Business Case for Integration — 85
- 8.6. Summary of Phase A — 85

9	Phase B: Developing the Implementation Strategy Through Objectives and KRI's	87
	9.1. Survey of Key Drivers	87
	9.1.1. Processes and Tools	88
	9.2. Develop Implementation Strategy Through Objectives and Key Indicators	88
	9.2.1. Causal Indicators	89
	9.2.2. Output Indicators	92
10	Phase C: Realising and Rooting the Benefits	95
	10.1. Step C1: Systemic Alignment	95
	10.1.1. Personal Alignment	96
	10.1.2. Group Alignment and Cohesion (Values Alignment and Mission Alignment)	98
	10.1.3. Structural Alignment	98
	10.2. Step C2: Value and Culture Awareness Programmes	99
	10.3. Step C3: Continuous Re-evaluation: Monitoring Change Towards the Hyper-culture	100
11	Concluding Comments	101
Appendix		*103*
Index		*105*

LIST OF FIGURES AND TABLES

FIGURES

Fig. 1.	Balancing Competing Demands Leads to Compromise.	49
Fig. 2.	Framing the Dilemma on an x–y Grid.	50
Fig. 3.	Charting the Dilemma.	51
Fig. 4.	Reconciling the Competing Demands.	52
Fig. 5.	The Meta Dilemma of Acquisitions.	54
Fig. 6.	Comparison of Own Culture (Light Grey) with New Business Partner (Dark Grey).	60
Fig. 7.	Second Example of an Organisation Culture Profile.	63
Fig. 8.	Building the International Team.	71
Fig. 9.	Deciding Before or During a Meeting.	73
Fig. 10.	Top-down Versus Bottom-up.	74
Fig. 11.	Current Versus Intended Future Position.	91
Fig. 12.	Personal Key Reconciling Indicators.	92
Fig. 13a.	Innovation: The Reconciliation Between Invention and Adaptation.	93
Fig. 13b.	Innovation: The Reconciliation Between Adaptation and Invention.	93
Fig. 14.	Companion App.	104

TABLES

Table 1.	The Three Phase Process.	38
Table 2.	Step Wise Activities for Phase A.	39
Table 3.	Step Wise Activities for Phase B.	40
Table 4.	Step Wise Activities for Phase C.	40
Table 5.	Elements of the Business Case.	42

Table 6.	Common Business Perspectives.	46
Table 7.	Extreme Choices for Globalisation.	47
Table 8.	Organisation Culture Types.	61
Table 9.	Examples of Frequently Recurring Dilemmas.	62
Table 10.	Further Examples of Frequently Recurring Dilemmas.	63
Table 11.	Different Paradigms of Use for the OCP.	64
Table 12.	180 Degree Profiling with the OCP.	64
Table 13.	Example Integrity Charter.	68
Table 14.	Example Ranking of Personal Values.	77
Table 15.	Credo of Reconciled Values.	78
Table 16.	Example Core Values Metaphors.	79
Table 17.	Animal Metaphors.	80
Table 18.	Example Four Part Charter.	82

ABOUT THE AUTHORS

Fons Trompenaars, PhD, is Director of Trompenaars Hampden-Turner (THT) Consulting, an innovative centre of excellence on intercultural management. He is the world's foremost authority on cross-cultural management and is author of many books and related articles. He is CEO of THT Consulting and Culture Factory and Visiting Professor at The Free University of Amsterdam.

Peter Woolliams, PhD, is Professor Emeritus of International Management at Anglia Ruskin, Cambridge, UK and is a Partner in Trompenaars Hampden-Turner (THT) Consulting and its technical subsidiary Culture Factory. He has collaborated and published jointly with Fons over some 25 years. He has worked with Fons to develop a whole series of diagnostic apps and profiling tools and cultural databases which have led to the creation of the intellectual property of THT Consulting.

RATIONALE FOR THE SERIES

The business environment continues to change ever more rapidly. Established practice is constantly challenged in our post-COVID-19, climate-changing, technology-driven world, leading to the further proliferation of digitalisation, new flexible ways and places of working, leadership styles, diversity, etc. All areas of business and management are finding that traditional frameworks for organisation design, marketing, HR, and other functional disciplines no longer provide models for best practice. Not only driven by such changes in the external environment but together with the differing value systems of younger generations, there is an urgent need to provide new frames of reference that can help formulate new business strategies whilst synergising with the career aspirations of the labour market.

The New Business Culture is a series of micro-books with each addressing an area of business and management that seeks to demonstrate how and where established traditional models and frameworks are no longer providing optimum frameworks for a purpose that informs the range of subject areas discussed. The authors offer new approaches that transcend convention.

In this series of volumes, each distils the essential elements of a key topic and retains focus and purpose and seeks to offer new approaches to overcome the limitations of existing practice.

The content and new concepts therein originate from the synergy between the authors' own fundamental research (including supervision of PhD students) triangulated with evidence and application from their extensive client base in their consulting practice (THT Consulting, Amsterdam).

Purchase of each volume in the series includes exclusive access to a corresponding companion app. Each app enables readers to explore the application of specific concepts in further detail for individual volumes and what it means for them and/or their organisation.

ACKNOWLEDGEMENTS

The authors wish to thank Alexander Crépin from crepinconsult.nl for his inputs and constructive discussions and help with some translations (Dutch-English) of some earlier ideas Fons had documented.

1

THE LIFE CURVE IS HERE TO STAY

Stakeholders/shareholders, chief executive officers, leaders, and students of management and business studies always come across the 'life curve' at some time, but with routine day-to-day demands, it gets lost to their background due to all the other challenges they face. But eventually it catches up with us all. Organisations go through several phases from birth, growth, maturity, and death like every living organism. However, in theory, organisations can be immortal contrary to live organisms. For immortalising their existence, organisations have to manage organisational growth processes successfully, faced by differing demands in multiple ways, including through alliances, mergers, and acquisitions.

Larry E. Greiner in his famous *Harvard Review* paper 'Evolution and Revolution and Organizations Grow and Develop' described his model for a series of five key stages through which organisations progress, but he failed to develop a crisis paradigm for the last phase of maturity.[1] In general systems theory, organisations are classified as 'open systems' – that is, systems that have external interactions with the environment. By virtue of being an open system, they develop mechanisms to monitor the external environment – competitors, evolving legislation, changing value systems of clients, customers and employees, technology, and worldly events. Organisations, like Darwin's natural selection, respond to such influences by evolutionary processes that seek to exploit such changes or nullify any damaging threats.

---

[1] Greiner, Larry E. (May–June 1998). "Problems faced by organizations as they grow and develop". *Harvard Business Review*.

VIGNETTE: EXAMPLES OF EXTERNAL DEVELOPMENTS AFFECTING ORGANISATIONS

The Swiss (mechanical) watch industry was caught unawares in the 1960s when all watches were mechanical and no country was producing the precise movements required for top quality timekeeping better than Switzerland.[2] They experimented with quartz, but feared its threat to their traditional advantages. There had been 1,600 watchmakers that by 1970s had declined to 600. In March 1983, the two biggest Swiss watch groups, ASUAG (Allgemeine Schweizerische Uhrenindustrie AG) and SSIH (Société Suisse pour l'Industrie Horlogère), merged to form ASUAG/SSIH in order to save the industry.

Kodak is often cited as a prime example of a company that failed to adapt to the shifting product life cycle, specifically the transition from film photography to digital photography.[3] Despite inventing the first digital camera, Kodak clung to its film-based business model for too long.

BlackBerry dominated the early smartphone market with its business-focussed devices, featuring full keyboards and secure email.[4] However, as the smartphone market entered the growth phase with a focus on broader consumer features like apps, touch screens, and multimedia capabilities, BlackBerry failed to adapt its product offerings quickly enough.

In contrast, other organisations were able to survive by merging.

---

2 The Quartz Crisis and Recovery of Swiss Watches | Relation Between Timepieces and Society. The Seiko Museum. Archived from the original on March 6, 2019. Retrieved March 3, 2019, from https://web.archive.org/web/20190306043210/ https://museum.seiko.co.jp/en/knowledge/relation/relation_11/index.html

3 Rees, Jasper (January 20, 2012). "The end of our Kodak moment". *The Telegraph*. London.

4 Timmer, John (December 2021). "The end of BlackBerry phones is finally, truly here". *Wired*. ISSN 1059-1028. Retrieved December 3, 2022.

> **VIGNETTE: EXAMPLES OF EARLY SUCCESSFUL MERGERS**
>
> In 1999, Exxon and Mobil, two of the largest oil companies, merged to form ExxonMobil, creating what was then the world's largest publicly traded oil company.[5] This merger allowed them to combine their strengths in various global markets, achieve economies of scale, and reduce costs through synergies, helping them to better survive the fluctuations in oil prices and the intense competition in the global oil market.
>
> In 2000, J.P. Morgan & Co. merged with Chase Manhattan Corporation, combining Morgan's investment banking prowess with Chase's strong retail banking operations.[6] The merger created a banking powerhouse capable of competing with the largest global banks, significantly enhancing their scale and scope in various financial services.

Survival can also be secured by acquisition rather than merger, enabling the acquiring company to either significantly enhance its core capabilities or diversify into new markets with great effectiveness.

> **VIGNETTE: EXAMPLES OF SUCCESSFUL ACQUISITIONS**
>
> In 2005, Google acquired Android Inc. for an estimated USD 50 million.[7] This strategic acquisition allowed Google to enter the mobile operating system market, which proved to be a game-changer. Android has since become the world's most widely used

---

5 Myerson, Allen R. (1998). "The lion and the moose; How 2 executives pulled off the biggest merger ever". *New York Times*. Retrieved April 15, 2024, from https://www.nytimes.com/1998/12/04/business/the-lion-and-the-moose-how-2-executives-pulled-off-the-biggest-merger-ever.html?pagewanted=all

6 Bagli, Charles V. (February 21, 2018). "Out with the old building, in with the new for JPMorgan Chase". *The New York Times*. ISSN 0362-4331.

7 Amadeo, Ron (July 21, 2018). "Google's iron grip on Android: Controlling open source by any means necessary". *Ars Technica*. Retrieved December 31, 2022, from https://arstechnica.com/gadgets/2018/07/googles-iron-grip-on-android-controlling-open-source-by-any-means-necessary/

smartphone platform, providing Google with significant leverage in mobile advertising and app distribution.

In 2016, Microsoft acquired LinkedIn for USD 26.2 billion.[8] This acquisition has been beneficial for both companies, with LinkedIn continuing to operate as its own distinct brand but leveraging Microsoft's resources to accelerate its growth and expand its business offerings. Microsoft has integrated LinkedIn's social network data with its cloud and productivity products, enhancing value for its enterprise customers.

However, these high profile successes are not the norm. Mergers and acquisitions often fall short of delivering their expected benefits for a variety of reasons, as discussed in more detail throughout this book. The complexities involved in combining two distinct business entities are immense, and various challenges can undermine the potential synergies and advantages originally envisioned.[8]

And of course, such mergers or strategic alliances are not just restricted to commercial companies. Local police forces seek to merge with neighbouring forces with the intention to exploit economies of scale. Regional and local government merge to form a single integrated entity. The UK government's VAT customs and excise department merged with the UK taxation department then called 'Inland Revenue' to form what is now called 'HMRC His Majesty's Revenue and Customs' department.[9]

And not only does survival involve large scale organisations, as private local coffee shops are bought out by chains such as Starbucks. Individual privately owned hotels and restaurants cluster into small groups of four or five and face the same challenges but often the same fate as larger organisation acquisitions.

---

[8] Greene, Jay; Steele, Anne (June 13, 2016). "Microsoft to acquire LinkedIn for $26.2 billion". *Wall Street Journal*. Retrieved June 13, 2016, from https://www.wsj.com/articles/technology-busiest-sector-in-merger-deals-this-year-1465861867

[9] UK, *Commissioners for Revenue and Customs Act 2005*, http://www.legislation.gov.uk/ukpga/2005/11/section/4

By 1905, when philosopher George Santayana[10] wrote, 'Those who cannot remember the past are condemned to repeat it', humans had already been gleaning lessons from history for several millennia. Around 800 BC, in the Iliad, Homer used the principal players in the Trojan War to explore leadership strategies and styles. Nearly 1,000 years later, at the start of the second century AD, Plutarch compared the character traits of historical leaders in Lives of the Noble Greeks and Romans. And of course, we are still at it today. Organisations blindly follow leadership and strategy lessons drawn from the lives of yesterday's inventors, tycoons, generals, politicians, and other leading lights.

Too many leaders in their organisation believe their survival is secure in spite of the fact that an organisations' past is no guarantee of its future. One day the product life catches up with you. Even the Dodo became extinct in 1681 in spite of aeons of evolution and simply seeking to merge or acquire (or be acquired) is not a simple solution.[11]

In this book, we seek to revisit the limitations of existing practice to mergers and acquisitions and offer new approaches based on our own extensive research – initially practitioner based whilst recalling Kurt Lewin's maxim that 'there's nothing so practical as good theory' to which we add 'there's nothing like good practice to develop new theory'.

---

10 Kinni, Theodore (2019). "Past performance is no guarantee of future results". Retrieved fromhttps://www.strategy-business.com/blog/Past-performance-is-no-guarantee-of-future-results
11 Baker, R. A.; Bayliss, R. A. (2002). "Alexander Gordon Melville (1819–1901): The Dodo, *Raphus cucullatus* (L., 1758) and the genesis of a book". *Archives of Natural History*. **29**: 109–118.

2

TIMES OF CRISIS

In the last few years, especially, there has been an increase in pressure on the needs for mergers and acquisitions (M&As). Given the changed context, the combination of the COVID-19 pandemic, energy, and geopolitical crises requires organisations to test their business operations and strategy for effectiveness and sustainability. This is nothing special because in an uncertain, rapidly changing world, organisations must constantly evaluate their business models and (re)define their service offerings to stay relevant and create value for (their) customers.

Critical assessment of the strategy, the core competencies, and the product and service portfolio has become a necessary and continuous process. Given the developments in the market, do they provide a sufficient basis for a successful continuation of the business activities, or is an adjustment necessary?

This way, growth opportunities can be identified promptly, and decisions about continuing structurally underperforming activities are completed on time. The recent crises have been boosting this process and causing business activities to be realigned rapidly. On the one hand, there will be divestments and disintegration processes. On the other hand, integrations and reorganisations will follow.

It is plausible that an accelerated farewell will be taken of insufficiently profitable or no longer strategic parts of the organisation. Although there is much scepticism in the market in these unusual times, there are almost always financially strong organisations or investment funds that now see the possibilities at home and abroad to make strategically interesting acquisitions of parties in serious trouble.

The latter is a development that cannot count on universal approval. In various countries, reference is made to the national or regional importance of 'own' strategic sectors and those foreign players should not take these over at a 'low price'. For example, in a recent report on European Union (EU) competition policy, mechanical, electrical, and plumbing enterprises (MEPs) emphasised the need to safeguard essential EU organisations and assets against hostile takeovers.

VIGNETTE: CONCERNS ABOUT CHINA'S M&A STRENGTH

Based on their research, Sachsenmaier and Guo[1-6] discuss that access to technology and know-how is one of the main reasons Chinese organisations invest in Germany. China uses acquisitions as an alternative to internal product and process innovation, learning from others instead of industrialisation based on internal innovation.

It ties in with 'Made in China 2025', the national strategic plan to develop the People's Republic of China's manufacturing sector further, starting in May 2015. This initiative encourages the production of high-quality products and services,

---

1 https://www.industryweek.com/the-economy/article/22024894/should-we-allow-the-chinese-to-buy-any-us-organization-they-want
2 https://justthenews.com/world/asia/made-china-owned-china-20-deals-show-how-china-gobbling-us-assets
3 https://www.mckinsey.com/~/media/mckinsey/featured%20insights/china/china%20and%20the%20world%20inside%20the%20dynamics%20of%20a%20changing%20relationship/mgi-china-and-the-world-full-report-june-2019-vfashx
4 https://www.forbes.com/sites/kenrapoza/2020/04/18/watch-out-for-china-buying-spree-nato-warns/
5 tps://www.foxnews.com/world/how-much-of-the-united-states-does-china-really-own
6 https://en.wikipedia.org/wiki/Made_in_China_2025

such as aerospace, semiconductors, and biotechnology, to help achieve independence from foreign suppliers. It is a blueprint to upgrade the manufacturing capabilities of China's industries from labour-intensive workshops to a more technology-intensive powerhouse.

Especially in the United States, President Trump and others are critical and oppose the development from 'Made in China' to 'Owned by China'. If Chinese organisations are free to acquire US organisations, especially in the energy or technology sector, they believe that this poses a significant threat to the rebuilding of US industry. NATO Secretary General Jens Stoltenberg recently warned of the risk of 'selling out' critical infrastructure to non-Western organisations in light of the COVID-19 pandemic. More and more voices can be heard calling for a more active industrial policy to protect Western technology against being bought by Chinese organisations.

The Chinese have a legitimate strategy of buying organisations to access knowledge and technology, of course. So do organisations in the West. However, it is often pointed out that there is no level playing field because the Chinese government restricts foreign ownership to several industrial sectors. Although this policy can be adjusted annually, the bottom line is that in most industrial sectors, it is only possible to enter into a joint venture with Chinese organisations. Another concern is the influence of the Chinese government on organisations. That influence can be used for geopolitical reasons. Recently, COVID-19 has made it clear that there are risks of relying too much on production capacity in a single country.

McKinsey researchers are signalling that we are all seeing trade disputes making headlines daily, that there is a tendency towards protectionism, and all this is happening when geopolitical tensions are mounting further.

According to the Boston Consulting Group,[7] strong parties have an extra advantage during a crisis. There is more room for the integration process because the competition needs a relatively long time to survive the crisis. So there is less attention to the competition. People are ready to start with full force as soon as recovery sets in.

> 'We manage our business as a portfolio and believe we are well positioned to invest, innovate, and balance risk and performance in any economic environment. This balance gives us a competitive advantage, especially when markets are transitioning or experiencing slower growth.'
>
> John T. Chambers,
> Chairman and Chief Executive Officer, Cisco Systems[8]

Be that as it may, whether it is about joining forces, increasing scale, or divesting, these are well-known strategies that come into play to survive even during an economic downturn. At such a moment, for many organisations, it does not happen out of luxury or the implementation of an existing long-term strategy but out of sheer necessity. In these circumstances, the success of the M&A process is more important than ever for the organisation's viability.

No organisation will remain the same if you evolve with the environment. The changes organisations face today are happening so quickly that it takes much work to respond to them with existing assets and resources. New impulses are needed, and then takeovers are seen[9] as an opportunity to catch up or take a lead.

---

7 https://www.bcg.com/publications/2020/covid-impact-global-mergers-and-acquisitions
8 "McKinsey: Conversations with global leaders". *McKinsey Quarterly* (July 2009).
9 Francois Mallette & John Goddard LEK Consulting, https://hbr.org/2018/05/why-organizations-are-using-ma-to-transform-themselves-not-just-to-grow

It is worth mentioning that COVID-19 has also led to problems in ongoing M&A processes. An example was the proposed acquisition of HAL's shares in the retail chain GrandVision by French-Italian eyewear giant Essilor Luxotica.[10] The whole deal was seen differently as visits to stores were limited due to COVID-19. This has led to lawsuits and an arbitration process. The billion-dollar deal was apparently in jeopardy. The atmosphere between the parties seemed spoiled. At one point, the CEO of significant shareholder HAL was not sad if that happened. He stated, 'Please let them walk away and give me that €400 mill' of the lump sum from the takeover.

Apart from the COVID-19 era, several factors are stimulating the M&A market. The first is that favourable credit terms are available to finance deals. Another factor has a demographic origin. This will pay off, in particular, for the small and medium enterprises (SME) market. Baby boomers want to retire and are willing to sell their businesses at a good offer or participate in leveraged buyouts by management. With the arrival of a vaccine and the change of power in the United States, there was also a positive perspective, according to Anu Aiyengar,[11] Global Co-Head of M&A at JP Morgan. 'M&A is a game of trust. With greater political certainty, the end of the pandemic in sight and strong capital markets, confidence in the C-suite and boardrooms is high. That bodes well for mergers and acquisitions' And President Trumps' re-election offers a quantum change in the business environment.

A survey[12] by the M&A Leadership Council in 2020 nevertheless indicated that the economic uncertainty of the COVID-19 pandemic is raising the bar for the teams that have to flesh out and implement M&A processes. A higher level of sophistication is required. More than before, the success will be in summarising the smaller details.

---

10 Essilor International moves forward with four worldwide acquisitions", http://www.healio.com. Retrieved July 19, 2024.
11 https://www.reuters.com/business/finance/jpmorgan-names-anu-aiyengar-sole-ma-head-after-albersmeier-steps-down-2023-01-12/
12 https://hbr.org/2020/06/what-ma-looks-like-during-the-pandemic

This is an interesting observation because the bar in M&A is already high. The integration processes are complex anyway and success is never guaranteed. Roger Martin once described an M&A as a sledgehammer in the *Harvard Business Review*, with typically 70–90% of acquisitions being a disastrous fiasco.[13] This image may be a bit dated, and the success rate would now be around 50%.

The percentages of success and failure depend on which source you consult and what has been researched as a measure of M&A success. In addition, there needs to be standardisation of how data from the various organisations are obtained, that is, the data sets are often not comparable. In addition, many M&A initiatives are being aborted and where the M&A deal is not concluded. These are usually outside studies. If we were to include this, the risks of M&A failures would be even higher.[14]

Research usually focusses on the development of shareholder value in M&A processes, but there are of course also organisations that are not listed on the stock exchange and for which this development is more difficult to monitor. Nevertheless, studies looking at shareholder value generally confirm that it is difficult to realise the intended value increase. For example, Global PMI Partners Benelux has established, based on a data analysis for the period 2010–2017, which the evolution of the market capitalisation of listed organisations after an acquisition generally leads to the destruction of shareholder value.[15]

If we assume that there is indeed a 50% chance that the M&A process will not bring what is intended, then that is a considerable risk, especially in a crisis period. There will then be much less fat and resilience to take a 'sledge hammer'. It is therefore not surprising that the bar has been raised higher.

It is also strange that there are so many M&A processes that do not achieve the intended success, especially when we consider that enormous amounts of money and resources are spent on acquisitions. The M&A world is a really big industry in financial

---

13 Martin, Roger (June 2016). "Abysmal failures". *The Harvard Business Review*.
14 "Investigating the deal making failure in M&A: Deal makers' perspective in Brazil", https://www.sciencedirect.com/science/article/pii/S0080210717301875.
15 https://gpmip.com/success-and-failure-in-ma-transactions-an-empirical-study/

terms. According to the Institute of Mergers, Acquisitions and Alliances (IMAA), since 2000, more than 790,000 transactions have been announced worldwide, worth more than USD 57 trillion. In 2018, the number of transactions had fallen by 8% to about 49,000 transactions,[16] whilst its value has increased by 4% to USD 3.8 trillion. Global M&As activity is booming, reaching USD 2.3 trillion in the first nine months of 2024 and counting ....

There is also much attention from academia and many academic studies examining the performance of organisations around and after a merger. Much is published about M&A anyway. The search term M&A yields more than 75,000,000 links on Google! According to Julia Bodner and Laurence Capron, the study of M&A and the complex process of M&A integration remains an area with many unanswered[17] questions.

Despite all this attention, no comprehensive approach still guarantees M&A success. This can be explained when one realises that every acquisition has unique characteristics, synergies, risks, and challenges. It is not about 'making the deal', but about 'making the deal work'. That is where the real challenge lies, because bringing together different national or, on a smaller scale, corporate cultures can quite easily lead to many misunderstandings for all sorts of reasons, with all the associated dangers.

> Peter Drucker once remarked[18] that the push for M&As stems less from good reasoning and more from the fact that doing deals is a much more exciting way to spend your day than doing the actual work.

---

16 https://imaa-institute.org/mergers-and-acquisitions-statistics/
17 Bodner, Julia and Capron, Laurence (2018). Journal of Organization Design. 7: Article number 3 (2018).
18 Cited by Jim Collins 2001, in *"Good To Great: Why Some Companies Make the Leap... and Others Don't"*, Random House Business; First Edition.

3

REASONS WHY M&A PROGRAMMES FAIL TO DELIVER THE ANTICIPATED BENEFITS

We list below an overall summary but will consider these in more detail throughout the body of the book.

3.1. CULTURAL CLASH

Cultural differences between the merging organisations are frequently underestimated and can pose significant challenges. Differences in corporate culture, management styles, employee morale, and operational practices can lead to conflicts, decreased productivity, and high turnover, which can sabotage the success of a merger.

3.2. OVERESTIMATION OF SYNERGIES

Another primary reason for failure is the overestimation of synergies. Companies often anticipate higher cost savings or revenue enhancements than can realistically be achieved. Integration complexities, unexpected costs, and operational disruptions can significantly reduce the anticipated benefits.

3.3. INTEGRATION DIFFICULTIES

The integration process is complex and fraught with challenges, ranging from information technology systems and operational processes to corporate governance and customer relationships. Poorly managed integration can disrupt business operations, alienate customers, and lead to significant inefficiencies.

3.4. HIGH COSTS

The costs associated with merger and acquisition (M&A) are often substantial and can include not only the acquisition price but also legal fees, consulting fees, integration expenses, and restructuring costs. These costs can erode the financial benefits expected from the deal.

3.5. INADEQUATE DUE DILIGENCE

Insufficient due diligence can lead to unpleasant surprises after the deal has been closed. Issues like overstated assets, undisclosed liabilities, legal issues, or overvalued target companies can turn what seemed like a strategic acquisition into a financial burden.

3.6. DISTRACTION FROM DAY-TO-DAY CORE BUSINESS

The focus on closing and integrating an M&A deal can distract management from the core operations of the business. This distraction can lead to neglected opportunities and weakened performance in the company's primary markets.

3.7. LACK OF CLEAR VISION AND LEADERSHIP

Success in M&A often hinges on strong, decisive leadership and a clear strategic vision. Absence of these elements can lead to unclear objectives, inconsistent policies, and misaligned goals between the merging entities.

3.8. MARKET AND ECONOMIC CONDITIONS

Changes in market conditions or economic downturns can also derail the expected benefits of a merger or acquisition. What might seem like a sound strategic move in a stable economic environment may become problematic in a volatile one. Imagine the horrors of merging in the imminent days of COVID-19!

3.9. REGULATORY HURDLES

Antitrust issues, regulatory approvals, and compliance requirements can delay or derail M&A transactions. In some cases, regulatory interventions can alter the terms of a deal significantly or add conditions that diminish its value.

3.10. LOSS OF KEY TALENT

Mergers often lead to uncertainty and anxiety amongst employees, prompting key personnel to leave the company. The loss of critical staff can impair the company's ability to achieve its post-merger goals.

3.11. COMMUNICATION ISSUES

Ineffective communication during the M&A process can lead to misinformation, anxiety, and resistance amongst employees and stakeholders. Ensuring everyone understands the rationale for the merger, the expected benefits, and their role in the new entity is crucial for success.

3.12. CONCLUDING COMMENT

When reviewing the above list, one can immediately see why successful M&A projects are challenging. Readers are likely thinking that with such a diversity of reasons, it is impossible to collate M&A's into a single unifying framework that can offer a greater chance of success. In fact, this is our mission in this book by offering 'new approaches' and new ways of thinking about M&A.

4

CONTEXT

4.1. THE DRIVE

The drive for global business expansion and development through mergers, acquisitions, and strategic alliances continues to be big business. And even in the (long) wake of 2008/2009, in the climate of banking difficulties and credit restrictions, more and more 'share for share' deals have been proposed and affected and this continues well post-COVID-19.

Mergers, acquisitions, and strategic alliances are increasingly pursued, not only to implement globalisation strategies and necessary restructuring, but as a consequence of political, monetary, and regulatory convergence. Global companies like P&G, Johnson and Johnson (J&J), IBM, GE, Pfizer, and Cisco, but also Tata & Sons, Mahindra & Mahindra, Haier, Lenovo, HSBC, and others all have a merger and acquisition (M&A) strategy coupled with an organic growth strategy to enhance growth and manage risk at the same time. Some will have partnerships with (former) competitors; others already pursue integrations with each other in particular markets or product ventures. Some have even outsourced or in-sourced particular capabilities to and from each other.

Circa COVID-19, M&As were at a historic low due to fears of an impending recession and rising interest rates. The total value of deals fell 37% from 2021's record high to USD 3.61 trillion, according to the Wall Street Journal.[1] This is the largest drop since 2001, when the value of global deals plunged 50% to USD 1.68 trillion.

At the beginning of 2023, companies have begun to adapt, changing the way that they structure deals to reflect changes in market demand to their advantage and minimise costs to the best of their ability, but many are still suffering the same fate in that the expected business benefits aren't materialising.

It seems inevitable that integrations will continue between smaller and larger entities for decades.

4.2. IT'S NOT EASY ...

Realising the business benefits and creating wealth in an integration process is difficult. After exploring M&A and integrations for decades, we still live with a record of about two out of three deals that don't achieve anywhere near the benefits that were initially anticipated. Although success rates of M&As are difficult to compare, as many surveys to this effect use a variety of metrics to assess success, most point to a success rate of about 1/3, where some pertain that only 20% of M&As are ultimately successful.[2]

Yet, these low success rates do not appear to have stopped the enthusiasm for organisations to grow by refocussing themselves through some integration.

Given the evolving global economic and financial climate, leaders of businesses worldwide have needed to manage their resources and assets tighter than before and build sustainable growth capabilities that withstand downturns and emerge stronger than before. Many pundits are projecting two conflicting trends, which started in 2009.

On the one hand, we observe a lot of divestments and de-integration processes going on, in particular, in the financial services industry. On the other hand, we see simultaneously a process of increasing

---

1 Cited in https://firmroom.com/blog/largest-recent-m-a
2 Booz Allen Hamilton study 2001 'Merger Integration: Delivering on the Promise', and KPMG M&A study report 1999.

integrations and reorganisations under pressure of global sustainability while global competitiveness increases.

Bigger companies will abound but their strength will lie in their nimbleness and agility, not simply their scale or scope, as many companies realise that they have to operate within a business ecology where interdependence, not independence or singular dependence, is the name of the game. Emerging markets will find more flexible capital sources and conglomerates will leverage and alter their strategic approach to markets forcing others to quickly adjust. We note that even big US-based companies employ more and more people outside of the United States and many generate more than half their income overseas (GE, Corning, IBM, J&J, etc.). Indian, Chinese, and South African corporations are acquiring and integrating companies in the United Kingdom, the United States, across various parts of Asia, and Africa (Old Mutual, Lenovo, Haier, Tata, Mahindra, etc.).

Constant change, economic waves, financial bubbles, ambiguity, and risk measures will put a greater emphasis on the ability to increase capacity and capabilities to influence employees, collaborate with other entities across borders and boundaries, and integrate with former challengers.

Leaders will require different competencies, as they are continuously faced with frequently recurring dilemmas or seeming trade-offs. Furthermore, leaders have to co-create solutions with their management teams and navigate their organisations in and out of complex strategic relationships with the ultimate goal of creating sustainable growth and value.

4.3. DEFINITIONS

It is constructive as a pre-cursor for our analysis to begin by reviewing different ways to define a merger, acquisition, or strategic partnership.

- An acquisition indicates one company buying another and integrating it into its organisation.

- A merger implies two organisations integrating into a third entity, even when the two original companies are of unequal size.

There are many varieties of these integration formats, and many that 'market' an outright acquisition as a merger in the public and/or private media.

- A strategic partnership or alliance may differ in this regard as there may only be an integration of a department or a smaller part of an organisation for a particular purpose or defined project. We have also witnessed strategic partnerships that eventually ended in a merger or acquisition.

For the purpose of this book, we will not overtly differentiate between these different types of integrations, but will focus broadly on the cultural challenges underlying any kind of integration between organisations with a common purpose or goal, whatever that goal might be. With that in mind, when we refer here to a merger, we include acquisitions, partnerships, joint project teams, and any other instance where people (re)organise themselves to forge relationships between human or organisational competencies with the ultimate goal to get more out of these relationships than the sum of their parts.

We approach the challenges of integration from the principle of creating value out of human relationships and its alignment with strategic intent.

4.4. OPTIMISM BUT STILL FAILURE

Over 20 years ago, KPMG (1999) and Booz Allen Hamilton (2001) reported[3] that more than 2/3 of mergers failed to live up to their own target, we have seen in our consulting practice some improvement in merger results in the past few years. The cynic would say that the main reason is that, because of financial scarcity, the prices to purchase have become more realistic. There are some reports indicating that the average price for the acquired company was 16 times Earnings before Interest Taxes Depreciation and Amortization.

---

3 Booz Allen Hamilton study 2001 'Merger Integration: Delivering on the Promise', and KPMG M&A study report 1999.

'A lot of organizations get so carried away with the idea that buying a smaller competitor is the fastest way to grow....

Integrating them quickly so they pull in the same direction can be a nightmare. This is often true so M&As go wrong.'
> Robin Booker, director of M&A consultancy Morphose[4]

PWC research assessing the experiences of more than 260 M&A deals in the 2014–2017 period shows that successful dealmakers excel in four areas: achieving synergies, completing integration within an ambitious timeframe, successfully managing culture and change, and implementing strong project governance.

It is also interesting to conclude that these four dimensions are strongly related: organisations that perform well in one dimension also do well in the other three dimensions. The report further concludes that organisations that put culture and change management at the heart of their M&A integration process perform better.

Thus, almost all organisations that live up to their culture and change management expectations also manage to stick to their original timelines.

Another report by PWC emphasises the importance of culture in M&A processes even more emphatically. It confirms that culture should be at the heart of the deal.

'It is fundamental to keep people and cultural aspects in the planning in advance.[5] Broad engagement and communication of the value creation plan will help maintain and build the buy-in of key employees and managers. Failure to plan for cultural change will significantly undermine the created value of the M&A deal.'

---

4 Cited by Hodge (April 2017). "Why do M&As fail?". *Risk Management Magazine*, https://www.rmmagazine.com/articles/article/2017/04/03/-Why-Do-M-As-Fail-
5 PWC report 2018, "Creating value beyond the deal", www.pwc.com/il/en/assets/pdf-files/2019/creating_value_beyond_the_deal.pdf

Although everyone experiences culture on a daily basis, not everyone is fully aware of the influence this has on our actions, on the way we interact with each other, and on how we approach things and come to decisions. What is considered 'normal' may turn out to be 'not so normal' during an M&A process ....

Still, anyone can understand that issues like this can arise when a foreign multinational listed organisation takes over a family business or a tech start-up just as this will be the case when a German or French organisation makes a takeover in the Middle or Far East. Many more examples illustrate that culture plays a major role in M&A processes.

It means that successfully integrating organisational cultures is not as self-evident as that one culture in which we function daily, let alone if you strive for 1+1>2.

Culture, therefore, requires a lot of attention both when entering into and when executing the M&A deal. On the one hand, methodical approaches are needed to clarify the similarities and differences. On the other hand, use those insights in a structured way to take the steps together to the intended 1+1>2.

> 'Culture is not just one aspect of the game. It is the game.'
> Lou Gerstner, former IBM CEO[6]

Based on the above, it should come as no surprise that the emphasis in this book is therefore on the 'soft' side of the M&A process with 'hard' consequences.

From our research, we find the human side, particularly the cultural dimension of M&A processes, both 'pre-merger' and 'post-merger' should receive much (more) attention or even be central.

At this level, there are complex problems and integration issues that need to be addressed. If this is not done promptly and with the right focus, cultural differences will inevitably lead to some or even major

---

6 Louis V. Gerstner Jr. (October 13, 2009). Who Says Elephants Can't Dance?: Leading a Great Enterprise Through Dramatic Change, Harper Collins e-books.

disagreement between leaders and stakeholders, reduced productivity, increased talent turnover, decreased customer satisfaction, etc.

It is all business with a higher risk of failure than complicated financial or technical issues. These can usually be solved with the right expertise and with an essentially linear, logical approach.

Anyone who is familiar with development and change processes knows that this is the 'soft' side, the difficult side, or as they say in English: 'soft is hard to do'.

Another finding from Roger Martin is interesting in this regard. He points out that 'organizations that focus on what they will get from an acquisition are less likely to succeed than organizations that focus on what they can give/offer'. These tie in with the idea that 'multiplication starts with sharing' .... In our opinion, valuable insights to keep in mind for M&A initiatives.

What drives us crazy is that especially buyers think that the only thing that matters to a seller is money and that they refuse to consider other things that influence the motivation of the sellers.

> 'One has to understand the people on the other side of the figure, their weaknesses, their strengths, and what motivates them if you want to get a trade done. Without it there is no discussion and no cooperation.'
> Ken Marlin, investment banker[7]

We have also gathered evidence that companies have become somewhat better at merging if they had realised the need to focus much more on the human factor, relationship management, communication, trust, and clear people process and human integration strategy.

More companies merging are doing just this now, and we have seen significant successes at IBM, Cisco, Compass (Catering), J&J, Linde AG, Vodafone, etc., but we'll have to wait for the results of Elon Musk's intervention with X, formerly Twitter.

---

7 Ken Marin blog: Retrieved from https://www.linkedin.com/pulse/marine-corps-way-win-wall-street-ken-marlin/

5

THE HARD AND SOFT ISSUES

Managing the key hard issues can in themselves determine the failure of a merger. These include:

5.1. FAILURE TO ELICIT AND FOCUS ON THE KEY ISSUES

5.1.1. Synergy and Savings Evaluation

Evaluation of synergy and savings for any merger or acquisition will confirm the direction the parties involved need to take and determine what steps need to be taken and which processes to be used.

This first step is crucial to provide the necessary reassurance during negotiation and early evaluation of the deal that the identified benefits are robust and can indeed be realised.

More specifically, the synergy and savings process evaluations generally focusses on the areas of procurement, R&D investments, and new product development, as well as distribution channel and supply chain analysis. Closer examination of the operation cost reductions normally considers the area of headcount reduction, which is often the most difficult synergy to achieve and implement.

Loss of staff is an inevitable outcome following the execution of a merger. What we learned from the KPMG (1999) study was that few companies move beyond statements of intent with regard to headcount reduction. As it is estimated that on average 50% of managers will leave following the first year of any acquisition or merger, it is important to precisely analyse how and indeed whether the vision, mission, and values of the 'NewBusiness1' are completely aligned within the merger strategy.

This important (re)alignment of business and cultural dilemmas forms the basis of our 'new approaches' to the integration process we consider in detail in this book.

Assessing the inherent dilemmas underlying headcount reduction becomes extremely important as well. The needs to elicit, recognise, respect, and reconcile the key dilemmas of a merger are dealt with in later chapters.

5.1.2. Integration Project Planning

The integration project planning process is the second most critical function as it is meant to form an expression of the manner the synergies from a combined organisation will be attained and give tangible evidence that things are stable yet changing. Project planning team member selection and goal setting communicate the strategy of the merger. This process is carefully monitored by the general employee population in the organisation, who are not directly linked to the integration process itself but merely subjected to it.

5.1.3. Due Diligence

Due diligence is of fundamental importance in the non-operational pre-deal activities as it enables the acquirers to focus their attention upon market reviews, risk assessments, management competencies, and synergies to support the operational impact. Generally, it does not involve a full review of the (corporate) cultures of the two companies, but stays within the realm of financial measurement and reporting tools.

5.2. FAILURE TO QUESTION (CULTURAL) ASSUMPTIONS

Generally and traditionally referred to as the soft issues, these challenges form the core around which we have created our human

5.2.1. Selecting the Management Team

Successful management teams for the NewBusiness1 require exceptionally strong and visible leadership and direction to drive forward complex value realisation.

Generally though, we find that such selection is either done in great haste (Bank of America and Merrill Lynch) with seemingly obvious power and title related choices, or too slow with a severe loss of motivation and morale which often results in the loss of important management talent, not to mention market value as investors grow impatient over time.

In this context, we need a stronger focus on the specific competences and skills of the leaders that initiate the merger and those leaders who form the integration management teams. These particular individuals need to be true reconcilers of differences and dilemmas of strategy, organisational structure, and team culture.

As such, we have found and will present a proven method to assess and train such individuals to identify the qualities of reconciliation of tensions and dilemmas which lead to integrated value at the organisational, team, and personal leadership level.

5.2.2. Resolving Cultural Issues

In most studies (including those we have cited), the main reason for merger failure is often attributed to 'cultural differences'.

Of course, we have to address these issues better and succeed where others have failed.

A rigorous, systematic, and triangulated approach to assessing cultural differences needs to be in place and communicated to the management ranks and beyond.

There are many tools in the market to help and we'll share a few of these in later chapters. But importantly, we have found that it is not just about measuring cultural differences and or resolving potential challenges. Our consulting process always starts with eliciting and prioritising the key integration issues through multiple assessments. The problem with organisational and national cultural issues in general is that the underlying basic assumptions remain largely implicit and under the surface. We have spent 25 years refining ways to make these cultural issues explicit and prioritise them. A major improvement of current integration processes can be obtained by using a consistent and well-researched method to elicit cultural issues, challenges, and dilemmas in a merger early on.

Crucial in this process is that the new culture to be created takes the best of all worlds and supports the new strategic challenges at stake. More on this important process is given later.

5.3. FAILURE TO COMMUNICATE EFFECTIVELY

Communication needs to be treated like any proper business process. It needs to be consistent, reliable, and repeatable. All leaders of industry know that any successful message needs to be repeated many times in many different ways. Yet, the underlying values and meaning (or culture) of the message need to be consistent, reliable, and repeatable. Management teams can never communicate too much although not to the point of 'crying wolf'.

As the KPMG (1999) report concluded: 'communications to employees will have a greater detrimental effect on the deal's success than that to shareholders, suppliers or customers ....'

Second level managers and lower level staff are often kept in the dark about the opportunities of the merger at their level, and are barely included in regular communications. To identify formal and informal ways to discuss and 'work', the communication channels throughout the merger process prove to be immensely important.

Those who prioritise communication plans as an all important part of their overall integration process are much more likely to be successful in attaining merger success than those companies that consider communication as one of a list of activities to be done in the chain of events.

Although in most surveys, the selection of the management team and resolving cultural issues generally score very high on reasons why mergers fail, evidence from our consulting reveals that the communications factor often acts as a multiplier for the first two factors in determining the success or failure of the merger. The ability to communicate effectively during a merger has become increasingly important as merging organisations face dilemmas.

Leaders need to create dilemma maps that elicit and analyse the toughest merger challenges and communicate a strategic path to reconcile these. These maps tend to integrate the need to build strategic alignment and commitment, while communicating a common language and supporting the vision. The dilemma maps become discussion models that lead to greater understanding, synergy, and alignment to reconcile the merger challenges amongst core project teams and other employees. We will elaborate on the power of these dilemma maps in detail later.

5.4. INTERIM CONCLUSIONS CONCERNING M&A FAILURES

What became evident from our own work on merger success is that each above-mentioned element has a primary role to play within the parameters of supporting the merger success and enabling its goal to be achieved. Yet, closer examination reveals that these key elements cannot maximise the potential benefit in isolation from each other because the activities must be brought together in a single integration process that enables the NewBusiness1 to maximise its post-merger success.

We conclude that a successful merger requires the exact same processes that any individual company requires. A vision and mission that indicate what we go for, a purpose that indicates what we stand for, a strategy that identifies how we'll get there, and values that direct us on how to influence the all-important relationships within and outside of our company to accomplish our goals.

As we will later review, we will find many dilemmas and challenges that ultimately personalise the merger process of the company and this is what keeps each corporation's merger process unique. We need to explore the unique culture and dilemmas that need to be elicited and addressed in each merger and provide a consistent, reliable, and repeatable process to drive its success.

5.5. MERGER GOALS

When we talk about successes or failures of mergers, we must address the measure of successes and failures of such mergers.

Most researchers tend to focus primarily on shareholder[1] value as the ultimate goal and measure of success of a merger.

But if we exclusively focus on the financial benefit of the merger and put a relatively short time frame for measuring the success of such a precise financial goal as the stock price and shareholder dividends, we are bound to deny various levels of complexity that provide a more sustainable shareholder value.

The richness of shareholder value as a single measure is such that it should not be disconnected from reaching various other, not insignificant, goals that substantiate a sustainable path or process towards continuing shareholder value of the NewBusiness1. Based on an extensive review of the management literature and interviewing thousands of international business leaders, our research shows that organisations face several five parallel goals at all times in their business cycle. These goals are contextualised by the ultimate goals of the organisations' vision and values, and the strategic purpose that supports this (see 1. and 2. below).

The remaining five represent the parallel aims of all organisations:

1. Achieving the (joined) vision.

2. Reaching our strategic goals after the merger.

3. Improving our overall business processes.

4. Reaching and continuing to be regarded as a 'best place to work' in our industry and beyond.

---

1 *Stakeholder value* also known as *equivalent for* non-governmental organisations.

5. Increase and maintain customer satisfaction ratings throughout the merger and thereafter.
6. Maintain and increase our overall contributions to society and general social, political, and economic recognition.
7. Which would all result in increasing shareholder value.

The notion of having these seven different goals is dealt with later, where we investigate the systematic and systemic approach to mergers by focussing on the dilemmas these parallel goals raise and the underlying value tensions that these dilemmas represent for the NewBusiness1.

6

INTEGRATED VALUE

6.1. BENEFITS BEYOND SHAREHOLDER VALUE

Organisations are commonly acquired on the basis of their inherent valuation (shareholder value) rather than with the intention of achieving full integration of all human capabilities.

Increasingly, however, we observe motives originate from a range of other expected benefits, including synergistic values (e.g. cross-selling, supply chain consolidation, and economies of scale) or more direct strategic values (to become market leaders, penetrating a readymade customer base, etc.).

The emphasis in the pre-deal and post-deal management, however, is too often focussed on seeking to quickly exploit the new opportunities under a mechanistic system or financial due-diligence mindset. It is assumed too often that delivering benefits simply requires the alignment of technical, operational, and financial organisational systems and market approaches.

The human relationships part of the merger is generally underestimated and few due-diligence methods assess the value of power and trust, or adequately map out the new and old stakeholder relationship management processes, inside of the newly created company structure as well as outside of it. We appreciate that this trend may change as the talent management teams are getting ready to take on more global roles and will have their strategic growth goals be linked to expansion and integration targets.

6.2. THE NEED FOR A NEW SYSTEMIC AND METHODOLOGICAL FRAMEWORK OF INTEGRATION

The evidence from our consulting experiences reveals that, next to paying an 'optimistic' price, the real underlying failure to deliver the anticipated benefits of mergers and integrations arises from the absence of a systemic and structured methodological framework.

Such a framework should focus on delivering the core value of human resources in business. How do we, in a dynamic way, assess the power of human interactions in the business context? The absence of a guiding framework means that senior managers do not know what to integrate or what types of decisions are important to deliver the anticipated benefits. Hence, these senior managers have no rationale to allocate human resources, prioritise actions, or achieve synergies, except as they match these against financial and capital resources. Yet, as we referred earlier, on a strictly financial or capital basis most merger and acquisitions actually lose money and destroy capital over time.

Simply measuring the financial value of the human resource is thwart with difficulty as humans are invariably more dynamic and versatile in comparison with financial or capital resources. Hence, it has proven elusive to measure the return on investment of human capital, although many have tried. The measurement itself is often a problem as well. How do you measure elements that are largely non-linear, intangible, and therefore tough to put on any metric scale in the first place, and subsequently measure the increase or decrease of their output over time?

Rather than attempt to measure the value of one human resource singularly in his/her ability to make a decision, we have established a more dynamic conceptual framework set on a dual axis grid of two opposing value orientations that holds the value orientations (current extremes) of the two partners.

7

OUR THREE PHASE FRAMEWORK

7.1. STEP BY STEP IN THREE PHASES

We will now explain our step-by-step process for aiding organisations in achieving the benefits of mergers, acquisitions, and alliances as developed from our on-going consulting.

It is essential to note that our approach goes beyond traditional change and project management. Our methodology includes specific tools and procedures that address key challenges to overcome obstacles that hinder the merger process. It is the culmination of all these activities that ultimately leads to success. We aim to offer the best practice, ideas, models, and experts to assure readers that many clients have tested and validated our ideas. We have designed these steps to be appropriate for the necessary stages of any merger, acquisition, or strategic alliance whilst considering our unique integration process.

Our cultural step-wise integration process is built on the philosophy that success comes from enabling people with different cultural perspectives to engage in meaningful dialogue. Our methodology, which as we stress repeatedly includes dilemma thinking, is central to bringing people together to discover shared values and differences.

At the meta-level, our research and practice show that successful integration requires the four components of:

1. recognition,

2. respect,

3. reconciliation of business and cultural dilemmas, and

4. realisation of the benefits of connecting different perspectives throughout the organisation.

Strategic, structural, systemic, human resource, supplier, and client processes must be aligned to achieve maximum performance. Our approach reconciles divergent goals, values, and structural, functional, and cultural differences.

The total 10-step process comprises three main phases (A–C) as listed in Table 1.

7.1.1. Phase A: Creating the (Compelling) Business Case

In the initial stage, there are five distinct steps as listed in Table 2. The first step involves redefining NEWORG's vision and mission, followed by formulating business challenges that arise from it as dilemmas that need to be resolved.

First, we will delve into the purpose and values that give meaning and motivation to the business case, making it more enticing. Then, we will establish a strong link between the performance and cultural issues, which will be the final step. Additionally, we will reiterate the exploration of purpose and values to emphasise their importance in the overall success of the business case.

Table 1. The Three Phase Process.

	A	B	C
Phase	Creating the (compelling) business case	Develop implementation strategy	Realising and rooting (the business benefits)

Table 2. Step Wise Activities for Phase A.

Phase A Activities	Goals	Means/Apps/Software Tools
Step 1: Revisit vision and mission	Truly integrated new organisation	Revisit mission and values with '4 whys?'
Step 2: Business assessment	Clarify new challenges through business dilemmas	Interviews validated by Dilemma Scan (software to elicit dilemmas)
Step 3: Values assessment	Define core values and key purpose for new integrated organisation	Interviews validated by Value Surveys (PVP (Personal Values Profiler) and OCP (Organisation Values Profiler) tools)
		Supporting workshop session to define key purpose
Step 4: Select supporting values and effective behaviours for business case	Linking values with effective behaviours	Online diagnostic Dilemma Scans
		IAP (Intercultural Awareness Profiler) and PAP (Personal Action Plan) tools + supporting interactive workshop(s)
Step 5: Assemble the business case for integration	Integrating business and values assessments for better business performance	Workshop sessions linking re-validated values with an effective business case

7.1.2. Phase B: Developing Implementation Strategy, Its Objectives, and Key Performance Indicators

During this phase, the focus is on designing a communication strategy that tailors the methodology and content of the cultural integration process to the needs of the executives. Personal feedback is also provided. The implementation strategy is developed along with clear objectives and performance indicators to measure progress as shown in Table 3.

7.1.3. Phase C: Developing Systemic Alignment and Value Awareness

This final phase involves aligning values with the vision and mission, making sure that everyone in the organisation is aware of this

Table 3. Step Wise Activities for Phase B.

Phase B Activities	Goals	Means/Tools
Step 6: Identification of key drivers	Design of the communications ~ customise the methodology and content of the cultural integration process, to provide executives with personal feedback	- Analysis of the PVP and OCP assessment - Coaching sessions - Workshops on the dilemma reconciliation process and developing key reconciling indicators (KRIs)
Step 7: Develop implementation strategy	Create clear objectives and indicators	- 'Causal' indicators that relate to values and behaviours - 'Output' indicators that relate directly to performance - 'Outcome' indicators that relate to the end results

alignment, and monitoring and controlling any changes towards the desired hyper-culture as shown in Table 4.

We can now take a closer look at each phase and its associated steps.

Table 4. Step Wise Activities for Phase C.

Phase C Activities	Goals	Means/Tools
Step 8: Systemic alignment	Alignment of values with vision and mission	- Individual and group cohesion workshops - Values to behaviour - Structural alignment of systems and processes
Step 9: Value and culture awareness programmes	Rooting awareness into the larger organisation	- Awareness/feedback against determined goals - Personal development: for example, blended learning through the ICP (Intercultural Competence Profiler) and our e-learnings
Step 10: Continuous re-evaluation	Monitoring (and controlling) change towards the hyper-culture	- Individual and group deliverables - KRIs (achievement of KRIs) - PAP progress and personal development reports

8

PHASE A: STEPS EXPLAINED

This requires the following:

1. Re(de)fine vision and mission.
2. Business challenges assessment.
3. Purpose and values assessment.
4. Choose/select values and behaviour.
5. Business case for integration.

8.1. STEP A1: REDEFINING VISION AND MISSION

A strong business case is crucial for successful integration. Integration becomes much smoother when all parties involved share a defined and compelling business case. Therefore, it's essential to establish a clear vision and mission for the newly integrated entity. Leaders should make their vision and mission explicit and refine them through extensive iterations to ensure they remain inspiring and motivating. Additionally, the organisation's shared values and behaviours should align with the established vision. This step aligns with the work of Collins and Porras,[1] who have shown that successful organisations require alignment between their envisioned future and core ideology, forming their vision.

---

[1] James C. Collins and Jerry I. Porras, "Building Your Company's Vision". HBR, Sept.–Oct. 1996.

A clear and compelling business case and a shared vision and mission are essential for successful integration as summarised in Table 5.

Core ideology, the yin in Collins and Porras' framework, outlines what an organisation stands for and its purpose for existence. In thriving organisations, the yin is unchanging and complements the yang, the envisioned future. The envisioned future is the desired state that an organisation aspires to achieve, create, or become. It necessitates significant change and progress to attain.

Numerous processes and tools are available to support the development of a new or renewed vision and mission. In this activity, it is crucial to revisit the envisioned future with a new leadership group and connect it with core motivation and business.

Since a vision is something that is discovered rather than predetermined, the exploration process is often an excellent way to communicate and explore the strengths of both organisations and how to integrate them without compromising. Additionally, it often reveals why an organisation was acquired in the first place. If the strategy is one of 'riding high', the self-confidence of the members of the acquired organisation is also boosted, including the essential commitment from the top.

The approach to formulating the vision and mission differed between UniCredit and Linde AG. Linde's chief executive officer (CEO) Dr Reitzle worked closely with the old board of BOC to redesign the process, which ensured that the whole board was committed and made a significant difference in the end.

Once the main vision and mission of the new company is defined, the organisation's leadership assesses its business and values. This is typically a top-down process, similar to the original decision that led to the merger or acquisition.

Table 5. Elements of the Business Case.

Core Ideology	Envisioned Future
Key purpose (why we exist)	A 10–30 year BHAG (big, hairy, and audacious goal)
Core values (what we stand for)	A vivid description
What do we stand for?/What are we going to do?	

Whether starting with the yin or the yang, the connections built between both are crucial. Often, the culture determines which end to begin with. Based on our experience, starting with the envisioned future and its included big, hairy, and audacious goal (BHAG) is more effective. It speaks to the executive's mind and initial concerns. Assessing the business logic of the integration early invites management to create a new, shared future and ask why they came together in the first place.

This approach works better than looking at differences first. Differences become more supportive of the integration process after shared boundaries are defined. This approach surfaces tangible issues resulting from differences and ultimately allows organisations to capitalise on differences, enriching the process.

Integrating diverse business and value orientations requires a joint effort in mutually understanding and reconciling differences, not one party trying to understand and adapt to the other. The integration process should focus on realising business objectives and solving joint business issues, rather than discussing differences for the sake of differences.

To create a vision for the future, it's important to start by defining the BHAG. A BHAG is a bold and inspiring mission that requires extreme effort to achieve, such as putting a man on the moon. According to the authors who coined the term, a BHAG should be clear, compelling, have a clear finish line, engage people, and be easily understood by everyone. It should also act as a catalyst for team spirit and be tangible, energising, and highly focussed.

Examples of BHAGs include becoming a USD 125 billion company by the year 2000 (Wal-Mart)[2] and democratising the automobile (Ford Motor Company).[3] To become the hub of digital engagement, Mark Zuckerberg in 2008 set the ambitious goal of reaching 1 billion active users globally by 2012 (Facebook).[4] Other BHAGs include

---

2 Jim Collins blog: Bigger, Better, Faster. Retrieved from https://www.jimcollins.com/article_topics/articles/bigger-better-faster.htm
3 from https://2012books.lardbucket.org/books/united-states-history-volume-2/s09-01-prosperity-and-its-limits.html
4 Sisi Caso, "The 10-Year Evolution of Mark Zuckerberg's Bizarre New Year's Resolutions". Observer Newspaper 1 September 2019.

making human life multi-planetary by sending people to Mars (SpaceX), to bring technology closer to humanity and enhance individual lives by providing consumers with easier access to technology that furthers their ability to create whatever they can imagine or dream up (Apple), and to bring digital information closer to humanity by organising world information using algorithms so that it can be used universally with ease, regardless of language barriers or technical knowledge barriers (Google).

These examples can assist you in getting started with aligning organisations around a single mission statement, which is a powerful tool. Additionally, they may be useful if you collaborate with your team to reset after achieving your 10–25-year goal as outlined in your vision statement.

Once a BHAG has been defined, the parties involved can explore areas of business synergy within the BHAG. The BHAG should challenge and compel all parties to work together as a team and give them a shared feeling of pride. It should not be a dreamy blue-sky ambition or a basic strategic goal, but rather a stretched goal that requires undefined and yet undiscovered forces to achieve. The top management team should work together in small subgroups to discover stretched goals for the BHAG.

8.2. STEP A2: BUSINESS CHALLENGES ASSESSMENT THROUGH CAPTURING BUSINESS DILEMMAS AND THEIR RECONCILIATION

> √ This is at the heart of our new approach and we therefore discuss in more detail.

When organisations merge, it's important to assess and support the integration process by defining business dilemmas in the context of the newly defined vision and mission. These dilemmas arise from competing demands of different stakeholders with differing interests and viewpoints. It can be a challenge to choose between hands-on or laissez-faire approaches, top-down or bottom-up management, and more or less centralisation. Choosing one option may mean giving up the benefits of another.

To elicit and capture these dilemmas, we conduct face-to-face interviews and use our online semi-structured questionnaire we call our Dilemma Scan. When different organisations with varying strategic and operational business orientations merge, it can be difficult to work together in a multi-organisation environment. Reorganisations after mergers or acquisitions can also affect the success of the new organisation.

A successful integration process requires recognising different business orientations, respecting differences, reconciling business dilemmas, and embedding business benefits throughout the organisation. For example, if a larger pharmaceutical company acquires a smaller firm to improve its innovation capabilities, it must reconcile the dilemma of increasing the size of the organisation for economies of scale versus maintaining the innovative powers of a smaller company.

When two organisations are merging, different stakeholders within each organisation may have different perspectives on the merger. Some common business perspectives that often arise during a merger are shown in Table 6.

These perspectives may sometimes conflict, and effective communication and planning are crucial for a successful merger. Addressing the concerns and interests of each group can help mitigate potential issues and challenges during the merger process.

The dilemma of centralisation versus decentralisation is common in many integration scenarios. The reconciliation of this dilemma largely determines the success of the merger. When a global organisation faces the choice between centralising or decentralising business activities, there are four possible extreme choices as listed in Table 7.

This new approach we have developed provides a unique method for solving such business problems that we call our 'dilemma reconciliation framework'. This concept helps organisations make strategic and operational decisions by analysing various options. Specifically, it helps organisations review their 'local' and 'global' orientations,

Table 6. Common Business Perspectives.

Executive leadership perspective

Growth and expansion	Executives may view the merger as an opportunity to expand their market reach and achieve growth objectives
Cost savings	They might be focussed on synergies and cost-saving opportunities that can result from streamlining operations and eliminating redundancies

Shareholder/investor perspective

Return on investment	Shareholders often want to see an increase in the stock price and dividends as a result of the merger
Market position	They may be concerned about the merged company's position in the market and whether it will remain competitive

Employee perspective

Job security	Employees are concerned about job security and whether there will be layoffs or relocations
Career development	They may be interested in how the merger will impact their career growth and opportunities within the company

Customer perspective

Service continuity	Customers want to ensure that the products or services they rely on will continue without disruption
Pricing and quality	They may be concerned about changes in pricing or the quality of products and services post-merger

Supplier perspective

Payment terms	Suppliers may worry about changes in payment terms or the possibility of losing a major customer
Long-term relationships	They might be interested in maintaining long-term relationships with the merged company

Regulatory and compliance perspective

Antitrust and regulatory compliance	The legal and compliance teams are focussed on ensuring that the merger complies with antitrust laws and regulations
Data protection	They may need to address data protection and privacy issues, especially if the merger involves sharing customer data

Organisation perspective

Centralisation	Headquarters often wants to see an increase in centralised standardisation after the merger
Decentralisation	They may be concerned about the merged company's position in the market and whether it will remain customised and flexible

Table 7. Extreme Choices for Globalisation.

	Explanation of choices
Centralise	This response is to centralised strategy. This is the 'head office' dictated paradigm
Decentralise	Another possible choice is to decentralise, that is, to 'go native'.
Compromise	Each side gives up something to achieve a common goal, that is, centralise some things and decentralise others.
Reconcile centralise and decentralise	Much more challenging ~ and at first sight not what one might think is possible. Key question is: What do we need to centralise in order to allow for more decentralised activities? As we discuss below, when two apparently opposing views are reconciled so that instead of an 'either–or' thinking, or 'and–and' thinking, there is a 'through–through' solution, where new value is created by combining the best of both

creating synergies that lead to better outcomes. This framework enables companies to integrate both centralised and decentralised strategies, which is the key to reconciling dilemmas successfully.

Mergers are a common source of business dilemmas, mainly when the cultures of legacy organisations differ for business reasons. However, when organisations approach dilemmas in a healthy manner that reflects complementarities, it is a sign of successful integration. On the other hand, the absence of dilemmas could be a cause for concern.

For example, one could be facing a dilemma regarding whether to supply global or locally tailored products and services. Furthermore, one needs to consider the competing demands between developing your people with the need to focus on delivering results. Reconciling these dilemmas is crucial to the success of the new joint venture.

Dilemma Hierarchies: When UniCredit integrated the German HVB and Austrian Baca organisations, they encountered a dilemma regarding whether to become a fully integrated European bank or maintain close local relationships with clients. This meta strategic dilemma gave rise to related dilemmas, such as centralised versus decentralised excellence and entrepreneurial flair versus clear codification

8.2.1. Our Recompilation Process: Reconciliation of Business Dilemmas or Assessing Integration Potential

This follows the following steps:

1. Identify the dilemma.
2. Chart the dilemma, making it more specific and labelling the opposing positions on the axes. Plot the positions of the actors.
3. Stretch the dilemma by describing the positives and negatives of each side.
4. Create epithets to characterise the sweet or sour in each extreme box.
5. Reconcile the dilemma by asking how Value A can support Value B and conversely, how Value B can support Value A.
6. Develop an action plan, considering obstacles and monitoring progress to root the implementation plan to secure the business benefits.

The following illustrates the steps:

> **VIGNETTE: DECISION MAKING DIFFERENCES?**
>
> When a German mining giant merged with a US-based mining company, the decision control exerted by the German leadership stifled US flexibility and autonomy.
>
> The US-based leaders wanted to execute a quick deal with another US entity that would have them buy much-needed technology and thereafter sell the mine to a third party in the United States. Their efforts were thwarted, as they required approval from the steady and slower German decision makers, who required input from several stakeholders, including the employee council.

Phase A: Steps Explained

The challenge in the above case can be stated as a dilemma between two desirable competing needs:

On the one hand	On the other hand
we need a fast decision-making process to benefit from rare market opportunities.	we need a secure and steady decision-making process to build consensus across various stakeholders.

The tensions that arise are normally seen as options in competition and give rise to discussion (arguments) about which is better. Going to one extreme loses the advantages of the other.

In conventional thinking, the more you give support to one side, the less you can give to the other. Trying to balance with some of each only leads to compromise, as indicated in Fig. 1.

Each extreme side of this dilemma thus creates a pathology of the underlying value orientation and does not constitute sustainable integrated value, as it rejects the other side entirely.

But let's adopt our new approach based on a new way of thinking, where most would call this 'wanting to have our cake and eat it'.

First, we need to move away from thinking in terms of a linear scale between the two extremes and instead frame them on an x–y grid as shown in Fig. 2. We then annotate each axis with the positives and negatives of each proposition (axis).

It is helpful to characterise the two extremes with an epithet, which is a cryptic phrase expressing the quality or attributes of the extremes.

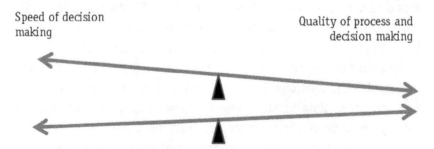

Fig. 1. Balancing Competing Demands Leads to Compromise.

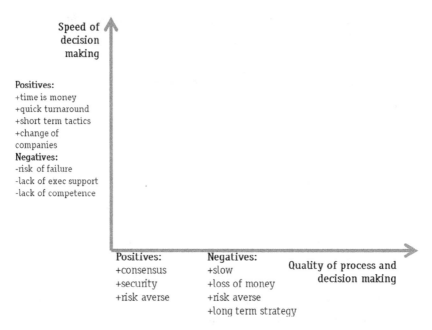

Fig. 2. Framing the Dilemma on an *x–y* Grid.

In this case, we chose to describe the extreme US value as 'Catch as catch can' and the German value orientation as 'High quality but late' (shown together with explanatory comments).

The mid *x* and mid *y* position is simply a compromise (something is lost from both extreme positives).

Those readers who have studied national cultural differences will be aware that the US Americans have more of a short-term horizon and will not be surprised that it was the compromise position on this grid is that actually happened. Yes, the US entity bought a third party and sold it on instantly to another buyer without further content benefit, but with a financial gain from the transaction.

But after this event, we helped the parties get together to frame and resolve the tensions that were created in the process of the deal. As both sides explored the dilemma, they quickly realised that the synergy of their opposing value orientations could have benefitted the company 11 times what they got out of the deal this time.

This is a fine way to start to calculate the synergistic value of human capital. When leaders are working from the same map, and

Phase A: Steps Explained

have a process to recognise, respect, and reconcile the challenges between them, integrated value can be reached and measured.

The above noteworthy example is based on two seemingly opposing value orientations. Such value orientations can be organised in differences/dualities, and as long as we pull dualities of value orientations together into 'couples' where both sides are stated positively, we can measure the current status of the tensions between the two seemingly opposing values and 'score' these on the dual axis grid.

Our mapping of the dilemma now looks like Fig. 3.

So, how can we have 'our cake and eat it' and get the best of both?

Here again, we are caught in the trap of linear thinking by the use of the word 'and' because of traditional stereotype education that continues to fail us.

We need to replace 'and' by 'through'. We can 'eat cake through eating it'. Enough of our metaphor, what are we saying?

We should ask ourselves, using what we call through-thinking:

How can we improve the quality of our executive decision-making process *through* speeding it up?

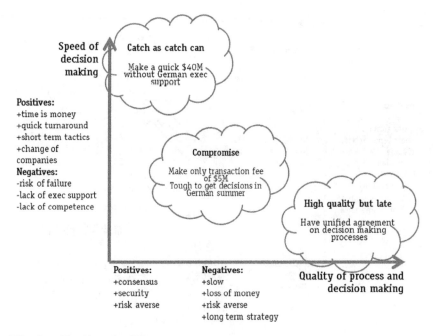

Fig. 3. Charting the Dilemma.

Or

How can improve the speed up our transactions *through* raising the quality of our decisions?

These reconciliations shown in Fig. 4 in fact gained another USD 55 million over and above the earlier compromise!!!!

We have created a 'library' of strategic and cultural, organisational, team, and individual dualities, which we call dilemmas. These dilemmas can be categorised along the lines of the dimensions of culture on the basis of which we have published extensively.

The principle of our new approach here is that values are differences and stem from tensions between two positive orientations/interpretations of this core value. Being able to dissect human activity and communication (decision making, negotiation, and presentation) and organise it's intent and results on a map created on the basis of seemingly opposing value orientations is not just of instructive, visionary, and motivational value but also a serious attempt to identify and measure the value of human relationships and trust in mergers and acquisitions (M&As) and many other reorganisations and human relationships.

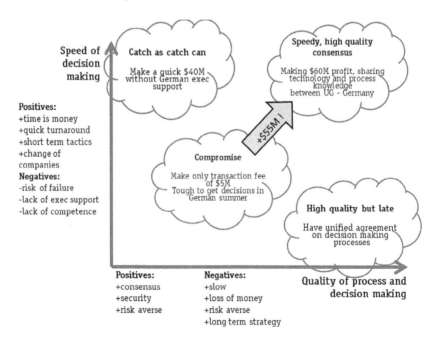

Fig. 4. Reconciling the Competing Demands.

Being able to map and measure a human integration approach in the context of complex organisational changes has proved invaluable to the process of ultimate value creation, for which human interaction is responsible. The competence to integrate and the ability to multiply this effort across an organisation in a consistent, reliable, and repeatable manner frequently leads to a competitive advantage for our clients.

8.2.2. The Meta Dilemma of M&As

Let's move up a level and see how this approach helps us at the higher meta level.

Throughout this book, we will be using our two dimensional logic to map integration challenges and so we discuss the above introduction to this new approach in more detail below.

We use our 10×10 x–y grid approach again in Fig. 4, following the same model as shown in Figs. 1–3, where both extremes are shown together with how they might be connected.

We offer explanations for the justification and benefit from this approach in more detail later (p. 48 et seq), but as an initial example, let's consider the meta dilemma that summarises two extreme paradigms of 'acquiring' or 'being acquired' in the following example map.

The 'Take over' axis is set against the 'Being overtaken' axis in a manner that instantly suggests that the two are not mutually exclusive and that either approach will not optimise the scenario.

If we regard the 'Take over' axis and take its logic to its natural extreme, we end up in the space currently occupied by the 'bear hug', which we could indicate as the ($x=1$, $y=10$) position on the grid. So first, we have the alliance in which one of the partners sticks to its own values and proclaims: 'My values first!' and 'I win, you lose!'

Following from the model shown in both Figs. 4 and 5, every extreme on these grids will be indicated by an epithet as a characteristic that includes a positive sense (such as a hug) countered by its negative extreme (being squeezed). Mapped in this manner, we note that every extreme becomes a pathology in itself. That is, the 'bear' culture acquired the 'unicorn' culture for its uniqueness, applying its 'bearish'

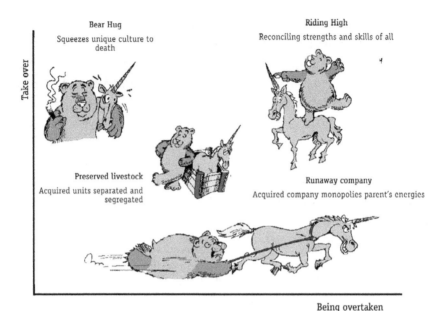

Fig. 5. The Meta Dilemma of Acquisitions.

ways will actually kill the unique features of the acquired company. We have seen this behaviour many times even since the late 1990s and during this century, when, for example, GM and larger pharmaceutical companies bought innovative companies. The GM way stamped out innovative, market directed ideas from the companies acquired.

On the other side of the grid, we identify the 'unicorn' culture running away with the bear behind it. The second type of response is to abandon your own orientation and go native. Here you adopt a 'When in Rome, do as Romans do[5]' approach. Acting or keeping up such pretence won't go unseen – you will very much be an amateur. Other cultures will mistrust you – and you won't be able to offer your own strengths to the merger marriage. Here, the acquiring organisation adopts the working practices and corporate culture of the organisation they acquire. Notice the anxious expression on the bear's face. Not exactly confident of its acquisition, is it?

Then there is the type of new partnership where a compromise between values is found. Sometimes adopting the acquirer's way of

---

5 Or more correctly, 'In Rome, do as the Romans'.

doing things, and sometimes the organisation being acquired. Synergies are not really achieved here. The middle ground (5, 5) outlines the concept of a 'compromise'. Both parties have agreed to play it safe and split the difference. There are many ways to arrive at this position of a stalemate, which we identify frequently as 'water with the wine', or 'a little bit of both'.

There is no benefit from the integration and no learning transfers from the acquirer to the acquired or vice versa.

Finally, and for mergers/alliances/integrations that are more effective and realise and exceed the expected benefits, we find the reconciling alliance in which values are integrated to a higher level of integrity, where both sides improve beyond themselves and synergise into a new entity with much higher valuation than the sum of its former parts. The extensive research evidence we have collected, and triangulated with real world application through our consulting, reveals that the 10, 10 paradigm in the top right corner is where a sustainable future that delivers the business benefits of the intended merger or alliance can be realised. The pathway to get there, we have named the dilemma reconciliation process.

Of course, there are many ways to get there and collect many excellent examples as well, guiding many client organisations to secure it.

IBM and PWCC performed an integration dance of change based on former CEO Lou Gerstner's book 'Who says elephants can't dance', implying that big blue needed to be nimble enough to tango!! For years, Cisco followed a different path, by quietly sneaking into its acquired companies and taking out the 'local' financial system and plugging in its own, leaving local management unperturbed and focussed on business development and sales. The global resource management power of Cisco now motored the local innovative business, and integration opportunities could be assessed on a financially even keel.

Our validated diagnostic questionnaires, structured interviews, and focus groups confirm that this new competency to deliver business success correlates highly with effectiveness in environments where one party needs to deal with diversity of values. In short, where parties can reconcile and integrate different perspectives (quickly), the expected benefits of the alliance or merger are achieved and even exceeded.

All cultures have their own integrity, which only some of its members will abandon. People who abandon their culture become weakened and corrupt. We need others to be themselves if partnership and any form of integration is to work.

This is why an approach that will reconcile differences is essential. Reconciliation enables us to be ourselves, but yet see and understand how alternative perspectives can help our own, whereby we improve ourselves. It is more than just avoiding mis-understandings through poor communication, and more than avoiding blunders. By connecting and using the strengths of BOTH parties, reconciliation generates the integrated value because both parties contribute TOGETHER.

Once players in alliances and mergers are aware of their own mental models and cultural predispositions, and once they can respect and understand that those of another (corporate) culture are legitimately different, it becomes possible to reconcile differences, yielding these positive business benefits.

Let's forge ahead and continue our complete integration process.

8.3. STEP A3: PURPOSE AND VALUES ASSESSMENT

After defining the desired future and assessing the business case and framing the overall meta dilemma, the next step is to conduct a comprehensive evaluation of personal, current, and ideal cultural values throughout the organisation. The suitability of these values must be determined based on whether they will contribute to the realisation of the organisation's envisioned future.

8.3.1. Finding Purpose

To effectively determine the purpose of the organisation, it is best to start with the larger context and ask the top group why they exist as a new entity. This is commonly known as the organisation's PURPOSE or its 'raison d'être'.

Initially, it may require some brainstorming to move beyond the goal of 'making more profit' or 'having more products to offer'. It is essential to reach the ultimate desired state without being afraid of exaggerating. The key purpose of an organisation is characterised by the following fundamental reasons for being: a guiding star at the horizon which we will ever pursue, what guides and inspires us, and what gives meaning to all the work one is doing for this organisation.

To find the purpose of the new (combined) organisation, one must think beyond everyday goals. If the organisation has no other aim than what it does daily already, there is no potential for growth, and there is a risk of standstill. Making profit and earning money should not be the highest aims of a company. Money should be like oxygen for a body, but when it becomes the main purpose, it can be detrimental.

8.3.2. Approaches to Discovering the Key Purpose

Discovering the (key) purpose of an organisation requires different approaches that can be applied separately or in combination. The most common way to elicit the key purpose can be the application of the '5 times why-exercise'. It involves asking why a particular statement is important and finding a more fundamental reason. Continued iteration challenges the weakness of any current statement to elicit the root definition ultimately.

8.3.3. Culture and Values

After crafting the mission and purpose of the organisation, it's time to explore its values. Values are the unique elements that support both the mission and purpose. They originate from these two factors and activate certain types of behaviour. 'Values' define what is good or bad, whilst 'norms' define what is right or wrong. Behaviours are simply expressions of these values and norms. For instance, the Dutch value consensus highly because they had to unite to fight against water. Similarly, the United States has many lawyers because

Americans had to be mobile and lacked time to invest in relationships. As a result, contracts and lawyers became essential. Swedes are forward-looking because they had to plan for the rest of the year during their relatively short summer. Their main economic source for centuries was forestry and wood processing, so they knew it takes 30–50 years for a tree to be replenished once it's been pulled down.

Organisational cultures also similarly develop their values and behaviours. Values help support an organisation's functions, and more importantly, they help organisations survive in a harsh business climate and achieve their goals. Values should be linked to the organisation's mission, not just a CEO's hobby horse. When two or more organisations merge, their deep values structure cannot be ignored. All values have a reason for existence, and this must be acknowledged. In our process, we take this as a starting point for the way forward.

Cultural diversity is expressed in viewpoints, values, operational priorities, and ways of doing things. In our experience working with organisations facing complexity caused by cross-border M&As, we have found that issues rooted in cultural differences can be formulated as dilemmas. This allows us to reveal how such tensions manifest openly. Since culture is a key human driver of organisational performance, people from diverse backgrounds offer different solutions to universally shared business topics. This leads to differences in management style, decision-making processes, communication styles, client orientation, reward mechanisms, and more.

Measurements: Our Organisation Culture Profiler (OCP) by M&A Scan

Organisational culture is essential to an organisation's success, as it provides a unifying theme that guides decision making, resource allocation, and response to the environment. Similar to an individual's personality, culture is a hidden yet crucial aspect that impacts the ability to handle challenges and dilemmas, especially during M&As.

To understand the values and cultures of existing organisations involved in a merger or acquisition, we utilise the M&A Scan. The M&A Scan provides users with a better understanding of and detailed

Phase A: Steps Explained

information on the differences across organisational cultures. It provides users with a new way of dealing with the tensions raised by different organisational cultures.

8.3.4. Why an M&A Software Diagnostic Scan?

This scan is intended to develop users' understanding of the importance of organisational culture by providing example stereotypes from different types of organisations. In spite of well-developed processes for due diligence, many M&As are still failing to deliver the expected business benefits due to clashes in organisational culture.

Readers can use a version of this scan[6] to explore our approach based on extensive research and consulting practice that integrates different cultures and harnesses the best of both.

This scan enables you to quickly assess your organisation's organisational culture and compare it with your new business partner organisation.

This diagnostic software tool helps identify similarities and differences between organisation cultures, enabling participants to review and interpret relationships with the organisation and each other. Unlike other diagnostic tools, the OCP goes beyond diagnosis and serves as a basis for reconciling key tensions arising from mergers, strategic change, diversity, and globalisation. It is also designed to be culture-free, applicable to diverse organisational cultures worldwide.

The OCP diagnoses organisational cultures of parties involved in the integration process and clearly highlights value dilemmas faced by the new group. It is an organisational culture scan based on formalisation and flexibility, hierarchy, and openness to the environment.

The model has four quadrants[7] as a result of two main axes: person versus task orientation and hierarchical versus egalitarian.

---

6 See Appendix for access to our MandA app.
7 We refer to this organisation culture model of ours in other volumes in this series for the relevant context. For example, what it means for recruitment (Volume 1) and what it means for flexible working (Volume 2).

The organisation's orientation towards task, strategy, mission, role, efficiency, consistency, power, human relations, involvement, person, learning, and adaptability can be represented by the four segments. As shown in Fig. 6, each sub-segment within these four segments determines the major orientations and see Table 8 for definitions of each quadrant. The App has undergone extensive formal research and field testing and triangulation with face-to-face and online semi-structured interviews.

Cross-validating questions allow us to verify whether opposites and contradictions within one organisational culture have been reconciled.

Our OCP covers all four quadrants and the reconciliation between them, showing how healthy an organisational culture can be. External validation against departmental or functional performance indicators shows that the higher the scores on all segments, the higher the score on the validating reconciliation questions correlates directly with the higher long-term performance of the organisation.

Our new approach, centred on our OCPs, focusses on the value of integrating opposing organisation cultural values into one and benefitting exponentially from this fusion.

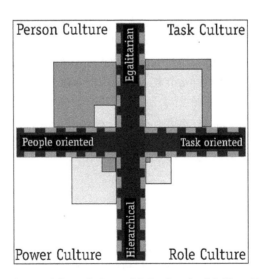

Fig. 6. Comparison of Own Culture (Light Grey) with New Business Partner (Dark Grey).

Table 8. Organisation Culture Types.

	Metaphor	Characteristics
Person culture	Incubator	• Management by passion • Power of the individual • Flexible working and easy to change • Professional recognition
Task culture	Guided missile	• Management by objectives • Commitment to tasks/results • Pay for performance
Power culture	Family	• Management-by-subjectives • Personal relationships • Loyalty, trust, team-spirit • Autocratic leader
Role culture	Eiffel Tower	• Management by job description • Expertise • Rules and procedures • Structural efficiency

For a more exhaustive analysis, we would normally recommend our more extensive Organisation Values Profiler (OVP) App based on some 46 diagnostics and responses collected from relevant employees across representative areas of the organisation – as well as data from your new business partner.

The conceptual framework and methodology are the same – namely, the identification of the competing demands that will arise from the respective corporate cultures which will manifest as dilemmas.

Realising the business benefits involves reconciling these important dilemmas so that synergy is obtained by harnessing the benefits of both organisations and avoiding extremes – such as the bear hug we have described earlier.

The OCP profile model in Fig. 5 was in fact the output from one of our clients involving a German pharmaceutical firm taking over a French organisation.

8.3.5. Tensions Revealed by Our OCP

If the comparison between your organisation and your new business partner suggests contrasts between the role cultured Eiffel Tower and the power centred family culture, then it is always important to consider which aspects of the Eiffel Tower should be retained and implemented. The challenge is to reconcile the tensions that arise from the differences between the culture types and not simply throw away everything from the past.

The main dilemmas likely to arise in this scenario are listed in Table 9.

If we take a second example of a large internationally operating consulting firm (see Fig. 7) acquiring a 20-person niche-consulting organisation, we see that the initial diagnosis revealed quite some dilemmas that emerged when showing the OCP's outcome. The comparison between the larger organisation and that of its new business

Table 9. Examples of Frequently Recurring Dilemmas.

Management:	*Reconciliation*:
Your organization would have a preference for authority that is based on formal titles from the right educational institute, whilst in the organization you would like to integrate with, managers authority is based on who you know and personal characteristics like charisma and dedication	Management needs to use their personality and charisma in order to make sense of their formal titles and education
Organizational logic:	*Reconciliation*:
Your organization's working environment would be based on the importance of being precise and reliable in the definition of efficient means versus the partner you want to join with would stress the importance of knowing people to get things done through relationships	Develop crucial systems and procedures, the executions of which is done by well-connected management
Motivation:	*Reconciliation*:
Your organization's working environment would be based on the importance of increasing expertise in doing a reliable job versus the partner you want to join with would stress the importance of long-term loyalty and commitment.	Members apply their expertise to the advantage of increasing the power of their colleagues
Decision making:	*Reconciliation*:
You would work in an environment where it is important to keep decisions focussed on getting the most efficient end result based on the involvement of experts whilst your partner organization would stipulate that decisions should be made by teams based on consensus	Have the most expert-driven and efficient decisions made by teams finding consensus

Phase A: Steps Explained

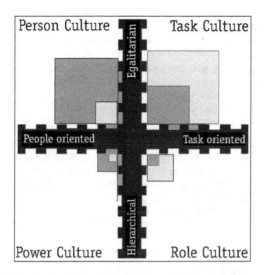

Fig. 7. Second Example of an Organisation Culture Profile.

partner suggests contrasts between the task centred guided missile culture and the person cultured incubator. It is always important to consider which aspects should be retained and implemented. The challenge is to reconcile the tensions that arise from the differences between the culture types, and not simply throw away everything from the past. When we are summarising them in the four categories of our M&A App we see the following differences as shown in Table 10 overleaf.

Table 10. Further Examples of Frequently Recurring Dilemmas.

Management:	*Reconciliation*:
Your organization (light grey) has a preference for authority that is based on the ability to get things done, whilst in the organization you would like to integrate with (dark grey), managers feel responsible for the development of creative individuals	Attribute the highest authority to those managers who have innovation and learning as prime criteria in their goals
Organizational logic:	*Reconciliation*:
Your organization seems to strive for a consistent goal orientation around the tasks you set as a staff member, whilst your potential partner organization suggests that the power of learning and creativity should be leading	Make learning and innovation part of the task description

(Continued)

Table 10. (Continued)

Motivation:	*Reconciliation*:
Your organization's working environment would be based on the importance of extrinsic rewards of a good job done such as a bonus versus the partner you want to join with indicates that an intrinsic reward like self-development would suffice	Describe task in terms of clearly described innovation outputs
Decision making:	*Reconciliation*:
You would work in an environment where decisions are made quickly for the benefit of getting the task done whilst your partner organization stipulates that it is important to keep on exploring more options even if decisions are not made or cancelled	Do continuous brainstorm sessions where, at the end, you decide what to do

In practice, there are different paradigms for which the OCP is used depending on the status/progress of the M&A initiative as shown in Table 11.

When the merger/acquisition partners know more about each other, 180 degree paradigms can give even more insights as shown in Table 12.

Table 11. Different Paradigms of Use for the OCP.

Looking for a new business partner	Compare your own organization culture with the type of organization you would like to acquire or merge with, or buy you
Considering a specific new business partner	Compare your own organization culture with the organization culture of an organization with which you are engaged in dialogue about an M&A programme
Post-merger	Compare your own legacy organization culture as it was before the merger/acquisition to what it is now in your new larger organization

Table 12. 180 Degree Profiling with the OCP.

Merger/acquisition in final stages of due-diligence	Respondents from Organization A describe their own organization culture and their perception of Organization B Respondents from Organization B describe their own organization culture and their perception of Organization A
Post-merger	Respondents from Organisation A describe their own pre-merger legacy organization culture in comparison with the new combined organization culture Respondents from Organisation B describe their own pre-merger legacy organization culture in comparison with the new combined organization culture

You can explore in the companion App the different main dilemmas likely to arise in different scenarios (see the Appendix).

8.3.6. Realizing the Business Benefits of the Merger/Acquisition

This quick assessment based on only 14 questions in our OCP App is limited in terms of more detail and we would normally recommend our extensive comprehensive OVP App based on some 46 diagnostics and responses collected from relevant employees across representative areas of the organisation – as well as data from your new business partner. (Again, the different paradigms in which this OVP can be sued are the same as for the OCP.)

The conceptual framework and methodology are the same – namely, the identification of the competing demands that will arise from the respective corporate cultures, which will manifest as dilemmas.

In the future, pundits[8] are predicting two conflicting trends: divestments and de-integration processes and increasing integrations and reorganisations under pressure from global sustainability and competitiveness. Organisations must operate within a business ecology where interdependence is the name of the game, and a single integration process that combines these key elements is necessary for success.

M&As often involve complex human relationships that should be considered more in the due diligence process. The value of power, trust, and stakeholder relationship management processes is not adequately assessed. This is expected to change as talent management teams take on more global roles and have their strategic growth goals linked to expansion and integration targets. Simplistic approaches to integration do not work in today's complex business world, leading to many mergers failing to realise the expected benefits. We have developed comprehensive solutions to help organisations achieve their maximum performance in the creation of a 'hyper-culture'.

---

8   For example, *Perspectives on transitions to sustainability*, European Environment Agency, Report, No 25/2017, ISSN 1725-9177.

We use a co-creation process with clients to tailor our consulting and leadership learning approaches to their specific needs, transferring this knowledge to clients so they can continue to benefit from it under their own leadership and management. Our approach is not just about avoiding conflict, misunderstanding, and embarrassment but also using differences to reach a higher level and deliver business benefits by connecting different cultural viewpoints. Leaders must continuously co-create with management and connect viewpoints that are difficult to reconcile.

We identify the underlying value orientations of these viewpoints and the natural tensions between them that need to be recognised, respected, and reconciled to obtain and realise the required benefits from the integration. One of the most important elements of integration success is a sense of urgency, executive leadership, and commitment. Our work leverages leaders' dilemma-resolution skills and applies a multiplier to this ability. As we have already stated, any genuine and successful integration process requires four components: recognition, respect, reconciliation (of both the business and cultural dilemmas resulting from these first two components), and realisation, in which the business benefits of connecting different viewpoints are embedded throughout the organisation.

The value dilemmas identified through these processes can validate the dilemmas raised by the PVP and OCP, and they are reconciled in the process described in more detail in later pages (p.48 et seq).

8.4. STEP A4: SELECTING VALUES AND EFFECTIVE BEHAVIOURS

To determine an organisation's core values, it is crucial to consider the envisioned future and key purpose. The selected core values should align with the organisation's goals and fit seamlessly into its key purpose.

There are various approaches to selecting core values, such as viewing them as integral actions, tools to reconcile business or cultural dilemmas, enablers of purpose and mission, or extensions of personal values. Each approach can help identify the organisation's most appropriate core values.

8.4.1. The Value of Core Values

Core values are essential to solving key business dilemmas and must be relevant and functional. They should support the process of dilemma reconciliation. The preferred approach is to identify the core values required to reconcile a dilemma and achieve the desired outcomes. For instance, UniCredit Group had faced several dilemmas related to its Italian character after acquiring the German HVB and Austrian BACA banks. The dilemma reconciliation process involves six steps that lead to various cognitive discussions around content. The seventh step requires participants to consider the values and behaviours necessary to support the action plan for resolving the dilemma. At UniCredit, visionary leader Allesandro Profumo had already established the core values but invited contributors to propose additional values and behaviours to reconcile the dilemmas. The resulting document, known as the *Integrity Charter*, ensured the validity and reliability of the core values (Table 13).

During the integration process, UniCredit invited participants of different nationalities to validate and translate the company's values into actual behaviour. As a result, the values became a distilled product of all the different banks and company cultures that have interacted with UniCredit over the years. These cultures share an unwavering commitment to market developments, added value growth, organisational social responsibility, staff development, and customer relationships. The six 'foundations of integrity' informed the behaviour of UniCredit people in their dealings with all counterparts, including institutional entities like government authorities and public officials.

The *Integrity Charter* is an impressive document, but like most moral statements, it contains omissions. Therefore, we need to qualify the original values without detracting from them. Values such as fairness, respect, reciprocity, transparency, trust, and freedom are

Table 13. Example Integrity Charter.

Dilemma	Values	Effective and Supporting Behaviours
Shared commitment: centralised versus decentralised excellence	Reciprocity, transparency, and trust	Alignment of the businesses by sharing best practices and improving communication on existing governance and processes
Transnational team: Italian versus other European cultural traits	Freedom and trust	Defining processes for talent development and recruiting consistent with key competencies and develop process to complement team diversity
Communication success story: 'AWARD' for champions managing diversity Meetings: ante-chambering versus equal opportunities to contribute	Respect transparency and trust	Golden rules for meetings, where accountability is clarified and leaders walk the talk
First mover: independence versus accountability	Reciprocity	Clear rules, standards and defined objectives, develop perimeter of competences and link to remuneration system
Walk your talk: proclaimed values versus opportunistic behaviour	Fairness	Develop people evaluation system, measurement of customer/people satisfaction, wide internal communication, and and emphasis on reputational risk
Communication: subtlety versus communicability	Respect, accountability, and transparency	Group meeting architecture with clearer rules on presentations and show discipline/consistency
Code UniCredit: entrepreneurial flair versus clear codification	Freedom, transparency, and fairness	Make heroes and visibly reward people, develop best practice sharing forums and reward sharing and distributing innovative ideas and allow for failures

abstract ideas, and their essence is what makes them essential. However, values tend to collapse when they accumulate like money in a bank. *To avoid this, we need to think of values in contrasting pairs since values are 'differences', not 'abstract things'.*

For instance, Arthur Anderson trusted Enron, and it ceased to exist. Because Anderson's job was not just to trust but also to verify through audits that Enron was trustworthy and then announce this to the world. Trust needs to have a relationship with supervision to grow together in integrity. UniCredit carefully applied their values to relationships, but they could go one step further and apply these to relationships between values espoused by different people. This same construct applies to all the remaining values in their list.

8.4.2. Conceiving Values as Integral Verbs

In the case of UniCredit, it is important to validate values by considering what values would help management reconcile business dilemmas. Management may also be asked to develop values that would be helpful in certain scenarios.

To illustrate, let's look at the 'Beauty' case where, as consultants, we guided the process to build a new organisation called PIOL. The main challenges faced were the push for cutting-edge products and unique services versus the pull of scalable and reliable ongoing services, offering globally significant services to an international clientele versus offering solid Dutch services to intimate clients, nurturing self-conscious and creative individuals versus developing teamwork, and continuous development of people versus contributions for shareholders.

When searching for values that could help tackle these dilemmas, initial attempts led to values that favoured one organisation more than the other. For instance, when client orientation was suggested, some consultants questioned whether it had to be a noun, and whether their cutting-edge services would be understood by clients. Similarly, the value of teamwork was criticised for potentially jeopardising autonomous creativity. Shareholder value was also questioned as to whether shareholders were being prioritised yet again.

However, the PI consultants understood the need for shareholder value as they invested at least 25% of total turnover in R&D, even during tough times. This was unsustainable, and it became clearer in their interactions with OL consultants who were used to less R&D investments and more dividends to their shareholders.

To connect these different points of view, we explained that values needed to be integrated with their opposites. They included the following values:

- striving for teamwork that consists of creative individuals,
- striving for local learning that can be rolled out globally,
- striving to develop leading-edge products and services that serve client needs continuously,
- and striving to develop shareholder value to further develop people.

Now, attention needs to be given to implementing these values and what behaviours would confirm that they are being lived in all sincerity. This is discussed later (p. 81 et seq) when we describe 'values to behaviour' (V2B) and key performance indicators[9] (KPIs) that can form the basis of monitoring take-up.

8.4.2.1. Values as Constructs to Aid the Reconciliation of Key Cultural Dilemmas

It's great to see all parties involved in vibrant discussions about functionality and working together towards a shared reality, rather than focussing solely on differences. However, cultural differences can still pose challenges and lead to potential problems if not addressed appropriately. We observed clashes between Italian and Germanic orientations during interviews with UniCredit executives, which were also confirmed by our OCP diagnostic scores. If these challenges are not overcome whilst respecting the strengths of each approach, the performance of NEWORG will continue to suffer.

To effectively address these cultural dilemmas, we suggest UniCredit build a comprehensive programme for growing its international rotational and expatriate workforce. This will help overcome any resistance to international assignments and ensure that the

---

9 As we shall see later, in fact, key **reconciling** indicators rather than simply key performance indicators.

company's future leadership is comprised of individuals with cross-boundary experience.

We identified several particular dilemmas that could have a significant impact on the effectiveness of UniCredit's meetings in NEWORG. It was recognised that UniCredit needed to reconcile these cultural dilemmas to ensure the success of the company's future endeavours.

The first was building trans-national teams, which requires overcoming resistance from local 'Old-Boy' networks and ambiguity around international assignments.

A related dilemma concerned Italian job opportunities and the need for more clarity and specificity in job descriptions to retain talent, as illustrated in Fig. 8.

The new management teams suggested a plan to resolve the dilemma, which includes the following steps: creating a 'wide talent programme' for Europe, systematically identifying and developing talents through fast-track programmes, providing cross-boundary opportunities for the best talents, formulating attractive expatriate policies, incentivising international assignments and expatriation, and formulating fair and attractive re-integration policies. They also recommended concentrating European-wide functions for expatriate career development at the headquarters, developing and implementing promotion and job posting policies that favour talent with international assignment experience, exploring dual incumbency with leaders from across boundaries,

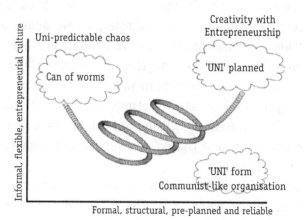

Fig. 8. Building the International Team.

supporting internal networking of talents, offering internet-based communication tools, encouraging bank-wide network directories, personal yellow pages, and more. The bank should attract external hires with the opportunities and projects that only a truly European bank can offer. Additionally, bonus programmes should be created to incentivise both own and cross-boundary cooperation success, and 'Blog'-like communication tools should be developed to create communities and peer group networking tools to bridge distance. To improve cooperation across boundaries, networking for all employees should be made a key priority. Regular face-to-face meetings should be conducted with sufficient frequency and lengths to foster the development of personal rapport and trust.

Another dilemma was identified in the way meetings were held and decisions were made. Italian executives would reach decisions by ante-chambering before meetings, which often left non-Italians feeling excluded from this very subtle and intimate decision-making culture. On the other hand, Austrian and German executives would prepare for meetings with agendas and detailed documents distributed beforehand to participants. The extant meeting culture was described as a series of discussions that served Italian executives to maintain pre-decision consensus. Italians expect actions on lengthy documents distributed at meetings, whereas Austrian and German executives expect that the meetings should focus on discussing the decision options during meetings. They expect decisions in meetings, and documents should have been distributed and analysed in advance. Many comments were added about the post-meeting implementation process. Italian executives expect that the decisions leave them degrees of freedom on how to implement, whereas Austrian and German executives want clear decisions with specific, well-defined actions. Germans will institute the solutions, whilst Austrians will instead find another solution they like more and implement that! This dilemma was mapped as shown in Fig. 9.

After conducting further follow-up meetings with the initial 60 interviewees, it was agreed that the following actions could help achieve reconciliation:

Phase A: Steps Explained

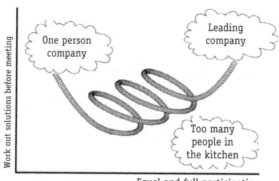

Fig. 9. Deciding Before or During a Meeting.

- Find volunteers who are willing to make the implicit communication rules explicit for each culture.

- Propose a reconciliation of styles that can improve the speed and quality of decision making, and have the management committee modify and approve it.

- Communicate the results.

- Create learning opportunities to acquire the skills for communicating in the cross-cultural communication style.

- Offer local co-facilitators from different cultures.

Another significant example of how the success of an organisation depends upon reconciling different value orientations is the leadership principle upon which the legacy Linde and BOC cultures based their delegation and accountability. Our OCP diagnostic revealed that Linde was a typical German 'Eiffel Tower' culture that lived up to the principle: 'Vertrauen ist Gut aber Kontrolle ist besser',[10] a famous expression often attributed to Lenin.

On the other hand, the guided missile culture of BOC, often organised in a project-like structure, was often led through delegation and management by objectives. Both orientations of top-down and

---

10 'Trust is good but control is better.'

bottom-up had their advantages and disadvantages, as shown in the following dilemma illustrated with cartoons in Fig. 10.

Many clients, including the top of the Linde organisation, have discussed the cartoon that depicts a common dilemma. This led to the idea of 'empowering people' and the understanding that a value is not a thing but a process in search of its opposite. The value is best captured by the supporting text: 'People are given the space to contribute and grow'.

There are several reasons why this value is important, including the fact that people create success and capable individuals can make a difference. Linde trusts its people and believes in empowering them to do the right thing. Key supporting values include accountability, trust, and transparency.

Behaviours that align with this value include setting clear goals and holding people accountable, defining boundaries but giving people space to take the initiative, encouraging entrepreneurship, standing up for what is right, supporting the development of people, and behaving consistently with foundational principles of safety, integrity, sustainability, and respect.

Linde rejects behaviours such as bullying, fear, and micromanaging. Therefore, 'empowering people' at Linde comes with account-

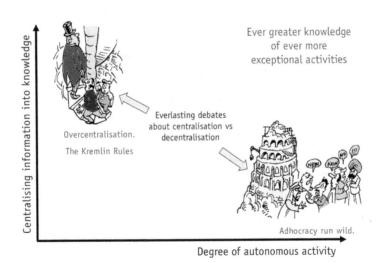

Fig. 10. Top-down Versus Bottom-up.

ability, trust, and clear goals, making it an integrative and successful value for this marvellous organisation.

Linde rejects behaviours such as bullying, fear, and micromanaging. Therefore, 'empowering people' at Linde comes with accountability, trust, and clear goals, making it an integrative and successful value for this marvellous organisation.

8.4.3. Values as Giving Life to Purpose and Mission

The Linde Group recently reviewed their values in comparison to their vision and founding principles. In a statement, their CEO, Dr Reitzle, explained that the merger of Linde and BOC a decade ago marked a significant moment for the company. Today, they are a global leader in gas and engineering with expertise in key areas such as energy efficiency, environmental protection, and healthcare.

Their vision serves as a guide for who they are and where they want to go as a company whilst their core values and foundational principles provide a framework for decision making and interaction with others. These values were identified through the participation of hundreds of employees and have been consistently agreed upon as the principles that should guide their actions and behaviour.

Overall, the values are viewed as the roots for Linde's vision, and they strive to continue making a positive impact on the world through innovative solutions and technologies.

8.4.4. Values as Extensions of Personal Values

In certain situations, established organisations may have too many conflicting histories and interests to form a clear set of values for the future. Rather than attempting to adapt existing values to fit the new company, we suggest that joint top leadership take our Personal Value Profiler (PVP) analyser App. This tool reveals the personal values of each leader and compares them to an initial set of values that they believe are appropriate for the organisation. Ideally, there should be a match between the two, as this is likely why they joined the organisation in the first place.

We use the PVP to validate the OCP and core values that are defined. In some cases, it is effective to start with the top leaders' personal values and reason from there. The Campofrio Group is a great example of this. In the beginning, the group consisted of many independently operating organisations throughout Europe. They attempted to define their values from the top-down:

> Our company values will center around a winning culture that is based on:
>
> - Responding quickly to customer and consumer needs
> - Adhering to quality and trustworthiness
> - Focusing on action and speed.

At the first meeting between all country heads and the European management team, it became apparent that people were uncomfortable with this approach. The core values were defined solely by the top leaders, and they were seen as too generic. However, they did serve a purpose in stimulating further discussion.

Responses we obtained from our PVP showed the following rank-order of personal values shown in Table 14. We categorised these into groups based on our organisational value proposition (OCP) database to create a conceptual structure.

We were pleased to find that the values were evenly distributed amongst the 12 segments of our extended organisational culture OCP model. Customer orientation, flexibility, open-mindedness, and entrepreneurial values were present in the three segments of the incubator, whilst reliability, consistency, and efficiency were found in the Eiffel Tower segments. Guided missile had decisiveness, focus, performance, achievement, and result orientation values, and trusting, committed, team orientation, and loyalty values were present in the three segments of the family culture. From there, we discussed which values would best summarise the essence of NEWORG by reconciling the business dilemmas to be resolved and the personal values of its leadership.

Table 14. Example Ranking of Personal Values.

Customer oriented	Most important
Reliable	
Flexible	
Decisive	
Efficient	
Entrepreneurial	
Performance driven	
Risk taking	
Achievement	
Innovative	
Result oriented	
Trusting	
Open minded	
Straightforward	
Committed	
Consistent	
Encouraging	
Energetic	
Focussed	
Loyal	
Team oriented	
Transparent	Important but less so

8.4.4.1. One Team, One Vision, One Mission

We had a very participatory process that reflected all the participants reconciling business and personal needs. The discussion was around what the new client group was sharing rather than all the differences that made up the organisation from the outset and were able to develop the credo shown in Table 15.

8.4.5. Exploring the Core Values of the Organisation by Metaphors

As a part of exploring an organisation's core values, we occasionally utilise metaphors with our Metaphor App. To do this, we request

Table 15. Credo of Reconciled Values.

Commitment:

We sustain our commitment with passion and talent, enabling us to deliver the best of ourselves and command the respect of all of our stakeholders. Our commitment is demonstrated every day in each decision and action, creating an environment that fosters achievement. It is an attitude that guides us and allows us to fulfill our role in the company responsibly. Commitment is the cornerstone of our success.

Relationships:

Relationships are the foundation of our business. We build relationships with each and every one of our stakeholders and the community at large over time, which are our most valuable assets. Respectful and sincere relationships drive preference and loyalty to our company by consumers, clients, suppliers, and employees. Relationships and teamwork that build on each partner's strengths are paramount for creating new opportunities to improve our business and sustain growth

Entrepreneurship:

Entrepreneurship at all levels will make us more creative, quicker off the mark, and bolder. It means taking initiatives in the relentless pursuit of excellence whilst respecting the established organisational objectives. Entrepreneurship is expected from each member of the company and provides us with first-to-market opportunities that energize our reputation and inspire the industry. Entrepreneurship is an attitude that defies the status quo, and when large corporations act like small businesses, the returns are immeasurable

Diversity:

Diversity leads to creativity and the development of groundbreaking ideas. It is a treasure that should be nurtured and leveraged in every discipline to accommodate different viewpoints and practices. Diversity allows us to think out of the box and to select and implement the ideas that will provide us with a competitive edge and sustained growth over time. Diversity gives each employee ownership of our successes. Diversity drives leadership

---

that leaders and managers select a car brand, animal, soccer team, and/or movie star that they feel is most closely associated with their organisation. We ask for metaphors that describe both the current state of their legacy organisation and the ideal state following a merger.

For instance, we recently conducted this exercise for a French and Dutch organisation that was merging. An example of the outcome is provided in Table 16.

A metaphor is a comparison between two unlike things, such as snow being like a blanket. The term comes from the Greek words meta, meaning 'above', and phor, meaning 'to carry'. Essentially, it is a way to carry a description above the literal meaning. Metaphors

Table 16. Example Core Values Metaphors.

Current	Ideal	Why?
10-year-old Range Rover	Toyota Prius (Hybrid)	Can cover all terrains, with great crossing capacity, but is heavy and expensive to maintain
A tractor	A new non-polluting bus	The system is weak, but it ploughs all the same
Audi A5	Volvo XC90	In general, we are well equipped for our task
Volvo	Toyota	Safe, structurally sound, boring, not trendy, and slow to react like a tank
Renault	Japanese equivalent	Pretty national, somewhat too traditional
Regular (gasoline) Toyota	Prius (hybrid Toyota)	Mass appeal to lots of people, but perceived as expensive
City bus	Four-wheel car	A lot of different people in it, all having different destinations

serve as a bridge between concepts, such as strategy, and our ability to reflect on them. They can also stand in for something we are trying to create, as aluminium cans stood in for Canon's disposable drums for home copiers.

For example, a team holding beer cans in their hands might be inspired to come up with a new idea. Or a paint company that imagined themselves as mountaineers on a vertical cliff face, hacking in the rock to get footholds, might be inspired to create a new product.

Metaphors suggest different patterns of relationships, which is why they are so valuable in this methodology. They encourage participants to detach from their current reality and come up with coherent analogies. Furthermore, values are integrated into a single animal that uses all the values in their relationships rather than just separate ones. By applying this methodology, people can conceptualise issues in a risk-free and depersonalised format and gain valuable insights into what they are thinking and what they believe.

Other examples from client participants where we as an alternative to motor vehicles, we used animals as the conceptual model as illustrated in Table 17.

Table 17. Animal Metaphors.

	Current organisation
Octopus	Intelligent species that survived through mutations over many years – but with a heavy head in the centre controlling what its tentacles do
	Ideal organisation
Racehorse	Well focussed, speed, and passion to win
	Current organisation
Antilope	Running around in a panic, not sure where to go
	Ideal organisation
Dolphin	Agile, flexible, fast, good orientation, living in groups, but enough space for some individualism
	Current organisation
Snake changing it skin	Evolving to the next stage, but which takes time, can be painful, and slow down the ability to react to changes in the environment whilst shedding its skin
	Ideal organisation
Hawk	Can see targets from a long distance and can move fast towards them. And does not have to fear enemies in its own environment

8.4.6. The organisation of Core Values

Having a set of core values is important as it provides guidance for an organisation. However, having too many core values can make it difficult to create a value-driven organisation. We have found it optimal to limit the number of core values to a maximum of four. It is important to translate these core values into tangible behaviours, which can then be communicated and implemented in the organisation's day-to-day operations, systems, and processes.

It should be noted that all core values are equally important without any priority order. These values are essential for the smooth running of the business, whether it is in meetings, making leadership decisions, dealing with employees, vendors, customers, or shareholders. The selected core values should be the underlying theme in any communication or action, representing the company's culture and supporting the strategic business case.

8.4.7. Translating Values into (Effective) Behaviours

Here we begin to translate constructs like values into what it means in practice on a day-to-day basis by identifying what behaviours are appropriate to bring about living the values. These include:

1. Giving direction to acceptable and unacceptable behaviours.

2. Imagining the future.

3. Making crucial decisions.

Whilst our online diagnostic web tools are focussed on diagnosing main differences between the key parties and individuals involved, this fourth step focusses on what the newly created organisation needs to share. It revisits the complete overview of the dilemmas that need to be addressed, both in terms of business and culture, in order to create a sustainable high performance culture in the post-merger process.

As we continue to say, the 'value' of a 'shared value' is the degree to which it helps reconcile the basic business and cultural dilemmas the organisation is facing whilst integrating towards its new organisation NEWORG. The quality of the joining of orientations that are not easily joined will determine the future performance of NEWORG.

So what does our combined organisation consider of value? Core values are based on what drives us and what binds us. Core values are the timeless tenets of an organisation. Together with its key purpose, it reflects what the organisation stands for and tells this story to the outside world.

8.4.8. Translating V2B: The Integrity Charter

Sometimes, management and other important staff members compliment the beautiful folders and brochures that express the organisation's core values and mission. However, these values are not always reflected in people's actual behaviours, leading to cynicism.

Two components can be used to define or refine the core values of the organisation:

1. The leadership group and their direct reports can participate in a dilemma reconciliation workshop to reconcile basic business and cultural dilemmas. This allows the selection of shared values and behaviours that help elicit actual reconciliation strategies.
2. After the first selection of shared (core) values, a V2B workshop needs to be run with the leadership group. The V2B process uses the organizations core values to re-establish trust, improve communication, and enhance cooperation and performance. The process involves creating a charter of behaviour that lists desirable and undesirable behaviours that are key to the effective handling of daily workloads and creating a positive work environment.

The latter involves translating every core value to desirable and undesirable behaviours using a structured worksheet. The team collects individual statements that are discussed and evaluated by the group. The end result is the selection of the most important core values for the leadership team, desirable and undesirable behaviours for the team, and the production of a charter (see Table 18).

Each team should practice what they preach by having a fun 'Living the charter' session!

Table 18. Example Four Part Charter.

Internal Charter of Behaviour

What members of the xyz team expect from each other

1. *Sharing* (to address the general lack of time and lack of support to prepare properly)

Supporting values	Observable behaviours	
Transparency	DESIRABLE: We want you to ...	UNDESIRABLE: We don't want you to ...
Openness	Exchange opinions and values	Make promises you can keep
Relevance	Visibly enjoy work	Take things too personally
Clarity	React to what I say	Make me believe you can do everything at once
	Respect people and show it	Act with no respect for the past
		Overwhelm me (leave the room)

Table 18. (Continued)

2. Predictable (to address the need for more trust)

Supporting values	Observable behaviours	
Trust	DESIRABLE: We want you to ...	UNDESIRABLE: We don't want you to ...
Responsible behaviour	Anticipate developments and share your vision	Tell different stories to different people
Sense of humour	Show respect for my ideas and solutions	Keep putting pressure on people
Accountability	Be open in all aspects	Let yourself be taken by surprise
	Live a decision	Put the blame elsewhere
		Be complacent

3. Team Play (to address differences in objectives and need for respect)

Supporting values	Observable behaviours	
Mutual respect	DESIRABLE: We want you to ...	UNDESIRABLE: We don't want you to ...
Assistance and help	State what you really think	Criticise team members without being supportive and constructive
Inspired management	Support weaknesses and stimulate strengths	Attack rather than reconcile
	Be interested in me and show it	Keep cards close to your chest
	Show empathy	
	Stay relaxed	

4. Improvement (to address too much functionality, silo behaviour and 'years of experience mentality')

Supporting values	Observable behaviours	
Creativity	DESIRABLE: We want you to ...	UNDESIRABLE: We don't want you to ...
Pro-activity	Focus on high-impact teams	Postpone tough decisions
Benchmarking	Share networks	Spend too much time on details
Creating win–wins	Develop the wisdom of where to go	Lose time on unrealistic deals
	Manage two levels down	Delegate to consultants
	Coach staff	

This overall 'V2B' mechanism harnesses the energy released by shared values within an organisation, particularly core values that embody its identity. However, these values often fail to inspire management and employees because they are too abstract to apply to real-life situations. To address this, V2B interprets or 'translates' values for their relevance in daily work, making the charter a vital tool for bringing them to life.

8.4.9. Intact Teams

This process is meant for teams that are still intact, with a maximum size of 20 people. The goal is to turn the translation process into useful behaviours that help the group perform better. An intact team is any group that shares common tasks and culture, and can be found at any level of the organisation.

Using intact teams for this V2B process is beneficial because team members can keep an eye on whether the desired behaviours are being expressed. This can be done during meetings, and it's helpful to have one team member check the behavioural aspect of the meeting and provide constructive feedback at the beginning and end. This role can be rotated amongst members.

The success of the process often depends on the homogeneity of the group and the clarity on the group's goals. It's common for individuals to be members of multiple groups. By living out effective behaviours, this process can lead to positive results.

The process of creating such charters usually takes about half a day, during which the team discusses implementation strategies, particularly how to track progress in behaviour. One option is to have one team member observe behaviour during operational meetings. Additionally, team members are encouraged to suggest a specific behaviour they want to focus on for improvement. These programmes have been highly successful and can be expanded to support staff and mixed account teams for larger clients. For the PIOL consulting company, this process resulted in a complete shift towards new values and behaviours, with past problems and ineffective behaviour becoming a thing of the past.

8.5. STEP A5: (REVISITING) THE BUSINESS CASE FOR INTEGRATION

This final step of Phase A aims to ensure that everyone is moving in the same direction. The leadership team has gathered enough information to create a detailed implementation plan. They have tailored their communication to align with the needs of the entire population and have a clear understanding of the collective vision, mission, core values, principles, and purpose. Additionally, they have established a set of behaviours and drivers that guide their daily decision making and actions.

Before initiating a whole system integration process that involves cultural change, it is crucial for the CEO and the board to clarify the compelling reason for integration. A clear link must be established between the performance issues and the cultural issues. The CEO and their team should present a convincing storyline to ensure that the reasons for the whole system integration and change are understood and supported by both the executive and employee populations. This is not only about improving current performance, but also positioning the company to take advantage of value differences and build long-term resilience and sustainability.

8.6. SUMMARY OF PHASE A

To summarise, the previous steps have established a clear joint visionary framework and purpose, identified cultural and value differences and similarities on personal, team, and organisational levels, highlighted the main business and cultural dilemmas that need to be reconciled, and identified the core values and behaviours that enable successful reconciliations. These ingredients are necessary to develop the second phase of the implementation of NEWORG's strategy, including key objectives and KPIs.

9

PHASE B: DEVELOPING THE IMPLEMENTATION STRATEGY THROUGH OBJECTIVES AND KRI'S

This second phase consists of two basic steps and begins to apply the results of the diagnosis and analysis undertaken in Phase A:

- Survey of key drivers.

- Develop implementation strategy through objectives and indicators.

9.1. SURVEY OF KEY DRIVERS

Our process of renewing an organisational identity involves reconciling differences in goals, values, structure, function, and culture. Our approach is to integrate strategy, structure, operations, people, and culture, whilst considering the economic, social, and cultural context of the organisation. Our goal is to optimise performance by aligning these elements.

Validation of key drivers is essential because it allows us to customise communication design, cultural integration methodology, and content, and provide personal feedback to executives and managers for coaching purposes. By objectively assessing the drivers, we ensure that we do not rely on assumptions. Additionally, the process of validating a key purpose and its core values helps align all participants in the process.

9.1.1. Processes and Tools

To provide context for the organisation's core values, the leadership team must validate the big, hairy, and audacious goal and 'key purpose' – the fundamental reason for being. The key purpose should serve as a guiding star that the organisation will always pursue but never fully attain. As such, it should not simply be imposed from the top down but co-created with the involvement of as many people as possible.

Since purpose and values guide and inspire the work done within the organisation, they should come from those involved and inspired. Once top executives draft the key purpose statement, it should be validated by those below. Therefore, the purpose must be expressed in simple language so it can be easily understood and improved through constructive criticism.

For example, after two iterations, the organisation proposed the following purpose statement to its top 200 meeting: 'Geodis Wilson is recognized as the best freight management service provider by customers, suppliers, and employees'. What do you think about this statement? What's good about it? What should be changed to improve it?

Another proposed purpose statement is: 'Deliver cutting-edge integrated freight management solutions to our customers and excel in our care for information, innovation, and consultation to be the best in class'. What do you think about this statement? What's good about it? What should be changed to improve the key purpose?

These discussions led to a lively, highly participative, and dynamic session where everyone felt involved and invited. The result was a sense of ownership and commitment to the purpose rather than feeling like it was imposed from the top.

9.2. DEVELOP IMPLEMENTATION STRATEGY THROUGH OBJECTIVES AND KEY INDICATORS

The chief executive officer and top leadership teams now possess enough information to create a detailed implementation plan. They have identified the compelling business reasons for the integration programme, customised communication, and determined key drivers for executives and employees. They have a clear sense of direction, including the vision, mission, and purpose, as well as shared core values and behaviours they aspire to, and a clear understanding of where all parties stand.

It is essential to establish targets for the integration process regarding both performance and cultural and leadership improvements. These targets should be captured in several indicators and represented in a variety of scorecards. However, the approach we take goes beyond 'balanced scorecards'. This is because as we continue to emphasise, balance implies that if you have more of one thing, you will have less of the other. This mindset is not useful when trying to create synergies between organisations. Instead, we aim to integrate differences and connect points of view, which we believe is a more effective way to facilitate implementation and enable post-holders to focus on delivering reconciliations. To achieve this, we use our 'integrated scorecard', which includes 'key reconciling indicators' (KRIs) *instead* of simple key performance indicators.

Adopting an approach centred around delivering SMART objectives would be counterproductive to the idea of reconciliation. In this scenario, we would only use dilemma thinking for diagnosis. However, by following an approach based on KRIs, we can bring the benefit of reconciliation all the way to the final achievement of a hyper-culture and mindset change.

We can categorise indicators into three types: 'causal' indicators that relate to values and behaviours, 'output' indicators that relate directly to performance, and 'outcome' indicators that relate to the end results.

9.2.1. Causal Indicators

Targets have been set to improve values and behaviour at both the group and individual levels. A balanced organisation cultural profiler (OCP) should display all four segments, demonstrating that key dilemmas have been reconciled and leading to high performance. PVP (personal values profile) and OCP are often used to monitor progress on behavioural and value levels, with cultural inertia decreasing every six months. The value to behaviours (V2B) charters are also referenced to see if intact teams and individual members are making progress on causal indicators related to values and behaviours.

The appraisal process must reinforce desired shared values and behaviours at an individual level. Checking the completion of previously agreed deliverables is insufficient because it lacks the behavioural component. The superior should also ensure that the individual's organisational activities align with the espoused values and behaviours. In more comprehensive approaches, team feedback on how the individual has lived the V2B process can be linked to this.

In the 'Beauty' case, introducing an integrated scorecard stimulated PIOL's integration process. The process started with a workshop where around 50 people gathered and recalled their values. Assessing whether these values are being lived cannot be done using a linear scale. Rhetorical questions appropriate to the values illustrate what needs to be assessed. KRIs are behavioural outputs that indicate that the value has been lived, and they should be specific enough and quantifiable if possible.

For example, on the first value, a KRI was based on invoices. On the local–global orientation, KRIs were formulated based on concrete examples of best consulting practices being communicated and used in the global network. On the push and pull dilemma, KRIs were designed based on co-developed services with the client and adapting the service according to client feedback. On shareholder value versus developing people, KRIs were adopted based on specific examples where the learning process has led to an actual increase in turnover and profitable consulting or training processes used to develop young junior consultants.

The process was effective in connecting different PIOL consultants to bind their strengths together. After the joint workshop, the process was installed on a web server for individual use by consultants and their superiors.

First, an individual consultant can score him or herself on a dilemma grid, indicating his/her earlier and later positions (typical screenshot, Fig. 11).

Phase B

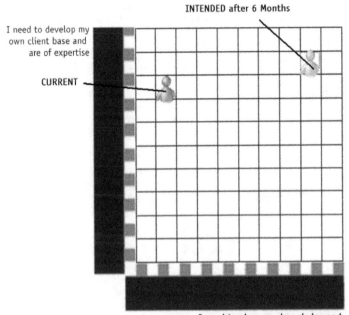

Fig. 11. Current Versus Intended Future Position.

For each dilemma, the respondent can propose and commit to three key KRIs. These KRIs are stored in an online database for future reference to track progress. This process, powered by the internet, also allows for updating the KRIs and suggests ways for organisational leadership to assist in making progress. And recently we have added artificial intelligence capability to provide further generative feedback.

The KRIs are signs that show to yourself and others that you have carried out the actions which are needed for the implementation of your reconciled solution to your dilemma. Respondents use the pro-forma shown in Fig. 12.

KRI examples:

> I can demonstrate to my team the benefits of the improved relationship with the customer.
>
> I will share the outcomes of the calls/meetings with my team on a monthly basis.
>
> The customers will buy an additional × amount of our new solutions.

Enter three KRI's you set for yourself and define the time frame within which you will have achieved the ideal position as you marked on the dilemma grid above:

KR:	Key Reconciled Indicator	Time scale (months)
KRI-1:		
KRI-2:		
KRI-3:		

Fig. 12. Personal Key Reconciling Indicators.

9.2.2. Output Indicators

We use output targets to measure performance improvement in areas such as productivity, efficiency, innovation, and employee and customer satisfaction. These measures must align with ongoing organisational monitoring.

Our unique approach to change management includes an online system that measures major dilemmas related to the above issues, as well as progress made by lower level groups in achieving reconciliations.

To provide empirical evidence for these propositions, we asked approximately 250 managers from various cultural backgrounds (mostly American and Danish) to complete our integrated type indicator (ITI), an extension to the classic meyers briggs type indicator (MBTI). The ITI explores how well a respondent can think and feel, not whether they think OR feel.

Our findings suggest that creative individuals move effectively between intuition and thinking, innovators publish their introverted calculation and continually learn by oscillating between judging and perceiving, and ultimately check their feelings through thinking. Culture often determines the extreme side that respondents start from, but it does not necessarily make one culture more creative than another. Combining opposite logics is essential for creativity, as clapping with one hand makes little noise.

Or graphically as illustrated in Figs. 13a and 13b:

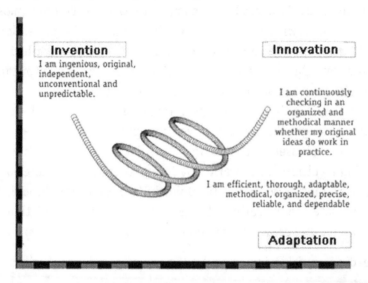

Fig. 13a. Innovation: The Reconciliation Between Invention and Adaptation.

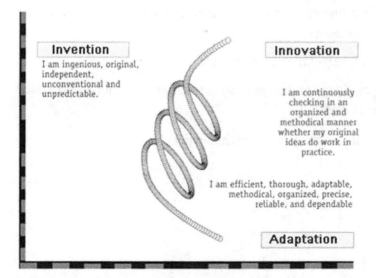

Fig. 13b. Innovation: The Reconciliation Between Adaptation and Invention.

After discovering that American professionals scored significantly higher in categories b (78%) and d (11%), whilst Danish professionals scored higher in categories a and c as expected, we initiated development programmes to cultivate a professional style of a (54%) and c (28%), resulting in increased innovation.

To accomplish this, we created a training programme that encouraged professionals across legacy companies to approach their (mostly R&D) dilemmas with a c or d mindset. Every six months, professionals had to complete the Integrated MBTI Questionnaire, which had four options, and this was validated by 360 peer review. This output indicator was taken as one of the main measures of progress.

This case highlights that the integration process can be easily guided through the right intervention processes, specifically the innovative mindset of the organisation. From there, we introduced building a culture of innovation by integrating the dominant Danish Incubator Culture with the US Guided Missile Culture through the intermediate Family Culture. In the first stage, this meant that the Danish and US operations worked on the following dilemmas:

- Leading participating employees versus respect for authority.
- Team spirit versus individual creativity.
- Effectiveness of teams versus creation of cultural knowledge about these teams.
- Lord, servant, or servant leader?
- How do we centralise lessons reaching us from decentralised locations?
- Social learning versus technological learning.

10

PHASE C: REALISING AND ROOTING THE BENEFITS

After completion of all the above activities, you will have arrived at the third and last phase that consists of the realisation and rooting of the previous activities:

1. Systemic alignment.

2. Value and culture awareness programmes.

3. Continuous re-evaluation: Monitoring change towards the hyper-culture.

10.1. STEP C1: SYSTEMIC ALIGNMENT

This process step aims to ensure that everyone is on the same page. The leadership team now has enough information to create a detailed implementation plan. They have identified compelling reasons for the integration, tailored their communication to align with the key drivers of the entire population, and have a clear sense of collective direction, such as vision, mission, core values, principles, and purpose. Additionally, they have established a set of behaviours to guide their daily decision making and actions.

The challenge now is to help the chief executive officer and the leadership team make the vision, mission, values, and behaviours pervasive throughout the organisation's culture in three steps. These steps include personal alignment, group alignment and cohesion, and structural alignment. The personal alignment and group-cohesion programmes aim to align the values of the top team and their direct reports (top 100 or so) with the vision and mission of the organisation. These executives are the guardians of the hyper-culture to be created. We have found that these programmes need to be integrated into the initiatives that the organisation has already established. In most cases, the personal alignment and group-cohesion workshops can be completed in two consecutive days. We herein provide examples of such programmes designed for the top three layers of the organisation.

10.1.1. Personal Alignment

We have taken the first steps towards aligning the personal values of the executive population with the core values of the new organisation. Our focus now is on implementing personal alignment programmes that support executives in understanding their core motivations and aligning their values with the newly defined shared core values. These programmes typically involve two-day workshops for intact teams with a focus on individual development. We use a variety of instruments as inputs, including the personal values profiler (PVP) and the intercultural competence profiler (ICP). Unlike other competence tools, the ICP assesses a complete spectrum of cross-cultural awareness and business benefits deriving from effective action in multi-cultural or international situations. We have frequently used our ICP to enhance the competence of leaders to take advantage of diversity in a merger or acquisition situation. The instrument comprises around 100 questions that are used in different combinations to achieve the total profile. We have confirmed the reliability of the combined integrated instrument through rigorous research and testing with MBA students, senior managers, and business leaders from our client base. Ratings are not simply added and averaged for different scales, but many sectors are computed from the root mean square quadrature of competing questions to assess their mutual interaction.

The ICP focusses on four aspects of intercultural competence.

- *Recognition*: How competent is a person to recognise cultural differences around him or her?

- *Respect*: How respectful is a person about those differences?

- *Reconciliation*: How competent is a person to reconcile cultural differences?

- *Realisation*: How competent is a person to realise the necessary actions to implement the reconciliation of cultural differences?

The ICP is completed online, generating personal feedback immediately. Upon completion, participants can download and save their personal profile report as a PDF file for archiving and/or printing. Additional basic biographical data of the respondent provide more extensive benchmark comparisons across the ICP database. Extensive feedback, extended interpretations, and theoretical background to the ICP are available in a series of interactive web pages at the web-based ICP support centre. Participants can explore their personal profile through these online tutorials that offer further insights, coaching advice, and suggestions for competence development.

Data collected have already demonstrated that the ICP profile provides an objective measure for the individual and organisation, revealing identification of the stage 'maturity' of the life-cycle phase. It identifies the relative imperatives for cross-cultural awareness training, the requirement to develop mindset changes and corresponding behaviour development for performance, through to achieving global business benefits by integrating cultural differences. Before and after measurements provide evidence of the impact of any intervention that can be correlated with improved business performance.

The ICP was developed because the limitations of our own earlier cross-cultural instruments that positioned people on bipolar scales of mutually exclusive extremes of seven dimensions were recognised.

The PVP is used to compare an individual's personal values with the core values and average scores of their organisation. This helps to clearly show any differences between personal and organisational values. The next stage focusses on helping individuals reconcile these differences through an enriching session that utilises the dilemma reconciliation process (DRP). Personalised coaching is offered to help participants develop a personal roadmap for integrating their personal values with their organisation's values. These coaching sessions also provide guidance on developing competencies for reconciling value differences across organisational, national, and functional cultures. These programmes are typically designed for the top three layers of an organisation.

10.1.2. Group Alignment and Cohesion (Values Alignment and Mission Alignment)

We next need to review and provide feedback to assess how aligned a business or functional unit's current culture is with the desired culture. We use our organisation value profiler (OCP) as a starting point to identify performance gaps and uncover underlying dilemmas. Our DRP session is then used to reconcile these gaps and provide a set of action points that link back to the core values of the organisation. Finally, we guide the intact group through an exercise on translating these values into their behaviour, following the value to behaviour approach explained in Step 4 for top leadership teams.

10.1.3. Structural Alignment

The structural alignment programme strives to realign the organisation's systems and processes with its vision, mission, values, purpose, and behaviours. This includes redefining key areas such as executive selection and orientation, performance evaluation and promotion criteria, appraisal systems, leadership development programmes, management training programmes, and value and culture awareness programmes.

10.2. STEP C2: VALUE AND CULTURE AWARENESS PROGRAMMES

At the organisational level, we replace personal alignment and group-cohesion programmes with a 'value and culture awareness' programme for lower tiers. The aim of this programme is to make employees aware of the significant differences in organisational and national cultures. We want to help them understand how these differences can advantageously contribute to the shared vision, core values, and purpose of the organisation. These programmes can be carried out in one- or two-day workshops, beginning with an introduction from at least two senior leaders. They will explain the importance of integration and outline the vision, mission, values, behaviours, and structural alignment programme. They will also provide specific objectives and key reconciling indicators (KRIs).

Our programme uses a 'blended learning' approach, where participants use tools like our web-based Culture For Business App. The assessment of individual value orientations through our intercultural assessment profiler is included in this programme. New organisation senior leaders review the results of the outputs/action points. Participants will learn how value differences and similarities can help achieve business goals. Using simulations and cases is essential to help them see how values, such as client approach, colleague treatment, and change management, can affect business approaches.

In international situations where understanding cultural differences is important for business effectiveness, we recommend setting up an Intercultural Competence Center. This centre can support the organisation's strategy through relevant intercultural training, consulting, and coaching initiatives. It can include country-specific workshops to increase awareness and competence to deal with specific national cultures.

The initiatives can be sustained by using theatre, storytelling, and artistic support like drawings and cartoons. This includes demonstrating undesirable and dysfunctional behaviours, etc. After increasing awareness, specific projects will be defined on how participants can contribute to the major dilemmas that the senior leadership has defined. These projects include topics such as brand image, corruption, promotion criteria for managers, quality improvement, diversity, etc.

Finally, it is essential to recognise that in some situations, starting with the values and cultural awareness programme is more effective than getting to the personal and group alignment programmes. To monitor progress, we develop a set of integrated scorecards that help guide and monitor the significant value tensions between personal, cultural, and core values.

10.3. STEP C3: CONTINUOUS RE-EVALUATION: MONITORING CHANGE TOWARDS THE HYPER-CULTURE

The pace and success of the integration process depend on the unique circumstances at hand. Tailored plans, interventions, and monitoring systems are necessary to manage progress effectively. As you progress towards complete preparation, you can use checklists to track implementation progress at the individual, company, and unit levels. These checklists can be incorporated into ongoing surveys, such as employee and engagement surveys. By combining progress checks with the reconciliation of main dilemmas and OCP and measuring KRIs in human resource systems, you can monitor progress regularly and make timely interventions.

11

CONCLUDING COMMENTS

As we said at the beginning of this book – 'it's not easy'.

We have sought to bring together our extensive practitioner led academic research with our theory led professional practice, leading to a rigorous structured step-by-step approach that gives serious consideration to the challenges involved.

Every culture has its own integrity, which only a small percentage of its members will compromise. People who reject their culture deteriorate and turn corrupt. If we want a partnership or any kind of integration to work, we need other people to be authentic. For this reason, a strategy that will bridge gaps is necessary. By allowing us to be ourselves whilst also seeing and understanding how different viewpoints can complement our own, reconciliation helps us to become better versions of ourselves. It involves more than just avoiding misunderstandings brought on by inadequate communication and mistakes. As we have tried to demonstrate throughout, reconciliation creates integrated value by bringing together and utilising the strengths of BOTH sides because both parties contribute.

It becomes possible to reconcile differences, yielding these advantageous business outcomes once participants in alliances and mergers are aware of their own mental models and cultural predispositions, and once they can respect and understand that those of another (corporate) culture are legitimately different.

It is crucial that the human part of the business operations is completely linked with their more technological and mechanical components in this process. It is perhaps too simple to explain why numerous experts from long-standing, major consulting firms have historically doomed NEWORGs to failure. These consultants frequently place a heavy emphasis on the mechanical, technical, and financial elements. Even whilst they now assert that they 'do culture', it is frequently treated as a side dish, which is the surest way to fail. But if one had only focussed on the outcomes of the human integration aspects, the failure rates would have inevitably been far higher.

Only when strategic, structural, human resource, supplier, and client processes are systemically aligned will the integration perform at its peak potential. Our new strategy is described in this broader perspective as a process of balancing opposing aims, values, structural, functional, and cultural variances for the best performance.

Whilst the press continues to report mergers that were disastrous, such as AOL and Time Warner (2000) costing USD 165 billion – often cited as the worst ever, it is not just the large conglomerates. Small family businesses such as coffee shops and restaurants that are absorbed into small chains continue to suffer the same fate.

Whilst such small and medium enterprises may not have the resources to undertake in detail all the steps of our three-phase process in full, even eliciting the key dilemmas and implementing their reconciliations rather than relying on a simplistic SMART[1] objectives model will help enormously.

As indicated at the beginning of this book, readers can now explore our organisation cultural profiler (OCP) App for themselves and test out different scenarios to elicit as described in the Appendix.

---

1 S (specific), M (measurable), A (achievable), R (realistic) and T (timely).

APPENDIX

TEST YOURSELF (OR YOUR ORGANISATION) WITH OUR ONLINE APP

You will have read that the authors are providing free access to a series of online WebApps that enables readers to explore the specific concepts in individual micro-books for themselves.

These are hosted on one of Trompenaars Hampden-Turner's (THT) Culture Factory's online web servers.

These WebApps will typically be shorter versions of the full online diagnosis (commercial) toolsets from THT Consulting. The aim will be to help the reader (after you have read the volume) explore the content contained in the text of this micro-book you have read to identify how the content relates to your own interest or situation.

This app also includes a podcast of author Fons speaking about mergers and acquisitions and a second podcast of Fons discussing the importance of values.

You will need a copy of the book to access the companion app (landing page as Fig. 14) for the specific volume. Surf to www.thenewbusinessculture.com, where you will be asked to locate a random word in the book, for example, the second word in Section 2 – and use this as your password. Each time the web portal is accessed, you will be asked for a different word and thus require a copy of the relevant book to hand.

Most of the WebApps are fully responsive and thus you can use a desktop or laptop PC, MAC, Android or IOS tablet, or smartphone.

Note we strongly recommend you access the app only after you have completed reading the full volume in order to derive the maximum benefit.

Dilemmas of Mergers and Acquisitions

Fig. 14. Companion App.

INDEX

Acquisitions, 4, 19
   realizing business benefits of, 65–66
Aerospace, 9
Allgemeine Schweizerische Uhrenindustrie AG (ASUAG), 2
Ambiguity, 21
Android, 3, 103
Antitrust issues, 17
Apple, 44
Assessing integration potential, reconciliation of, 48–53
   balancing competing demands leads to compromise, 49
   charting dilemma, 51
   framing dilemma on x–y grid, 49
   reconciling competing demands, 52

Baby boomers, 11
'Bear' culture, 53
Behavioural levels, 89
Behaviours, 57, 74
   conceiving values as integral verbs, 69–75
   effective behaviours, 66–67
   exploring core values of organisation by metaphors, 77–80
   intact teams, 84
   organisation of core values, 80
   translating V2B, 81–84
   translating values into (effective) behaviours, 81
   value of core values, 67–69
   values as extensions of personal values, 75–77
   values as giving life to purpose and mission, 75
Big, hairy, and audacious goal (BHAG), 43–44
Biotechnology, 9
BlackBerry, 2
'Blended learning' approach, 99
'Blog'-like communication, 72
BOC, 75
   cultures, 73
Boston Consulting Group, 10
Broad engagement and communication, 23
Building trans-national teams, 71
Business, 20, 24, 28, 81
   balancing competing demands leads to compromise, 49
   benefits, 61
   benefits of merger/acquisition, 65–66
   business perspectives, 46
   challenges assessment through capturing business dilemmas and reconciliation, 44–47
   charting dilemma, 51
   ecology, 21
   effectiveness, 99
   extreme choices for globalization, 47
   framing dilemma on x–y grid, 49
   meta dilemma of M&As, 53–56
   models, 7
   operations, 101
   recompilation process, 48–53

Index

reconciliation of business dilemmas, 48–49
reconciling competing demands, 52
synergy, 44
Business case, 38, 41–42
  elements of, 42
  revisiting business case for integration, 85

Causal indicators, 89–92
Centralization, 45
Chief executive officer (CEO), 42
Chinese organizations, 8–9
Circa COVID-19, 19
Cisco, 19, 55
Clear vision, lack of, 16–17
Client process, 38, 102
Co-creation process, 66
Co-developed services, 89
Communicate effectively, failure to, 30–31
Communication, 30, 52, 95
  issues, 17
  strategy, 39
Competition policy, 8
Complexities, 4
Compliance requirements, 17
Comprehensive approach, 13
Constant change, 21
Consulting process, 30
Context
  definitions, 21
  drive, 19–20
  optimism but still failure, 22–25
Conventional thinking, 49
Core ideology, 42
Core values, 76
  animal metaphors, 79
  credo of reconciled values, 78
  example core values metaphors, 79
  of organisation by metaphors, 77–80

organisation of, 80
value of, 67–69
Corporate culture, 13, 15
COVID-19, 9, 11
  era, 11
  pandemic, 7, 11
Crisis, 7
Critical assessment, 7
Critical function, 28
Cross-border M&As, 58
Cross-boundary cooperation success, 72
Cross-cultural awareness training, 97
Cross-cultural instruments, 97
Cross-validating questions, 60
Cultural clash, 15
Cultural differences, 15, 24, 70
Cultural dilemmas, 28, 70
Cultural diversity, 58
Cultural integration process, 39
Cultural issues, resolving, 29–30
Cultural predispositions, 101
Cultural step-wise integration process, 37
Culture, 24, 57–58, 81, 101
  awareness programmes, 99–100
  determines, 43
  factory's online web servers, 103
  measurements, 58–59
Current integration processes, 30
Customer orientation, 76
'Customs' department, 4
Cutting-edge integrated freight management, 88

Danish Incubator Culture, 94
Data, 97
Day-to-day core business, distraction from, 16
Decentralisation, 45
Decisive leadership, 16
Desktop PC, 103
Development, 19
Digital engagement, 43

Index

Dilemma reconciliation framework, 45
Dilemma reconciliation process (DRP), 67, 98
Dilemma thinking, 37
Distraction from day-to-day core business, 16
Drive, 19–20
Due-diligence methods, 28, 35

Economic climate, 20
Economic conditions, 17
Economic downturns, 17
Economic waves, 21
'Eiffel Tower' culture, 73
Emerging markets, 21
Employee morale, 15
'Empowering people', 74
Energy, 7, 9
Enthusiasm, 20
Entrepreneurial values, 76
Environments, 55
Envisioned future, 42
European Union (EU), 8
European-wide functions, 71
Exploration process, 42
Extant meeting culture, 72
External validation, 60
ExxonMobil, 3

Face-to-face
    interviews, 45
    meetings, 72
Facebook, 43
Financial bubbles, 21
Financial climate, 20
Financial scarcity, 22
Flexibility, 76
Ford Motor Company, 43
French organization, 24

GE, 19
Geopolitical crises, 7
German organization, 24
Global business expansion, 19

Global companies, 19
Global M&As activity, 13
Global organization, 45
Global PMI Partners Benelux, 12
Global resource management power, 55
Good theory, 5
Google, 44
Group Alignment and Cohesion, 98
Group-cohesion programmes, 95
Group-cohesion workshops, 96
Growth opportunities, 7

Hard issues
    due diligence, 28
    failure to communicate effectively, 30–31
    failure to elicit and focus on key issues, 27
    failure to question (cultural) assumptions, 28–29
    integration project planning, 28
    interim conclusions concerning M&A failures, 31–32
    merger goals, 32–33
    resolving cultural issues, 29–30
    selecting management team, 29
    synergy and savings evaluation, 27–28
Headcount reduction, 27
High costs, 16
HMRC His Majesty's Revenue, 4
Human activity, 52
Human competencies, 22
Human interactions, 36, 53
Human relationships, 22, 35, 52
Human resource, 36, 38, 102
Human trust, 52
Hyper-culture, 65, 95
    monitoring change towards, 100

IBM, 19, 55
Implementation strategy, 39
    causal indicators, 89–92

development through objectives
    and key indicators, 88–89
output indicators, 92–94
reconciliation between
    adaptation and invention, 93
reconciliation between invention
    and adaptation, 93
Inadequate due diligence, 16
Individual consultant, 89
Industrialisation, 8
Ineffective communication, 17
Information technology systems, 16
Inland Revenue, 4
Institute of Mergers, Acquisitions
    and Alliances (IMAA), 13
Intact teams, 84
Integral verbs, conceiving values
    as, 69–70
    building international team, 72
    deciding before or during
        meeting, 73
    top-down versus bottom-up, 74
    values as constructs to aid
        reconciliation of key cultural
        dilemmas, 70–75
Integrated scorecard, 89
Integrated type indicator (ITI), 92
Integrated value
    benefits beyond shareholder
        value, 35
    need for new systemic and
        methodological framework
        of integration, 36
Integration, 22, 41
    complexities, 15
    difficulties, 16
    process, 12, 16, 28, 43–45, 67,
        89, 94, 100
    project planning process, 28
Integrity, 55
Integrity Charter, 67–68, 81–84
Intercultural Competence Center, 99
Intercultural competence profiler
    (ICP), 96–97
Interesting observation, 12

Interim conclusions concerning
    M&A failures, 31–32
International business leaders, 32
Internet-based communication
    tools, 72
IOS tablet, 103
Italian job opportunities, 71

Johnson and Johnson (J&J), 19

Key cultural dilemmas, values
    as constructs to aid
    reconciliation of, 70–75
Key driver
    processes and tools, 87–88
    survey of, 87
Key performance indicators (KPIs),
    70
Key purpose, 88
Key reconciling indicators (KRIs),
    89, 91, 92, 99
Kodak, 2
Kurt Lewin's maxim, 5

Laptop PC, 103
Latter, 7
Leaders, 21, 31, 41, 66
Leadership
    group, 82
    lack of, 16–17
    team, 85
Learning process, 89
Linde Group, 75
Linde organization, 74
Linde rejects behaviours, 74–75
LinkedIn, 4
Local government, 4
Local police forces, 4
Local–global orientation, 89
Loss of staff, 27

MAC, 103
Management styles, 15
Management teams, 30
    selecting, 29

Market
  capitalization, 12
  conditions, 17
  volatility, 20
Medium enterprises, 102
Mental models, 101
MEPs, 8
Mergers, 4, 19, 47
  goals, 32–33
  realizing business benefits of, 65–66
Mergers and acquisitions (M&As), 7, 10, 16, 19, 52
  communication issues, 17
  cultural clash, 15
  distraction from day-to-day core business, 16
  high costs, 16
  inadequate due diligence, 16
  integration, 13, 16
  lack of clear vision and leadership, 16–17
  Leadership Council, 11
  loss of key talent, 17
  market and economic conditions, 17
  meta dilemma of, 53–56
  OCP by M&A scan, 58–59
  overestimation of synergies, 15–16
  process, 12, 24
  regulatory hurdles, 17
  shareholder value in, 12
  software diagnostic scan, 59–61
  world, 12
Metaphor App, exploring core values of organisation by, 77–80
Microsoft, 4
Mission, 31, 77, 89
  alignment, 98
  redefining, 41–44
  values as giving life to purpose and mission, 75
Mobile operating system market, 3

Money, 56
Motor vehicles, 79

National cultural issues, 30
NATO Secretary General Jens Stoltenberg, 9
'NewBusiness1', 28
NEWORG, 71
  vision and mission, 38
Non-operational pre-deal activities, 28
Non-Western organizations, 9

OL consultants, 69
Online
  diagnostic web tools, 81
  system, 92
  WebApps, 103
Open systems, 1
Open-mindedness, 76
Operational disruptions, 15
Operational practices, 15
Operational processes, 16
'Optimistic' price, 36
Organisation Culture Profiler (OCP), 60, 89
  degree profiling with, 64
  different paradigms of use for, 64
  examples of frequently recurring dilemmas, 63–64
  frequently recurring dilemmas, 62
  by M&A scan, 58–59
  organisation culture types, 61
  second example of, 63
  tensions revealed by, 61–65
Organisation Values Profiler App (OVP App), 61, 98
Organisation(s), 1, 5, 35, 56–57, 65
  approach, 47
  of core values, 80
  core values, 87
  leadership, 42
  mission, 58

PURPOSE, 56
senior leaders, 99
Organisational competencies, 22
Organisational cultural issues, 30
Organisational cultures, 24, 58–59
Organisational identity, 87
Organisational level, 99
Organisational value proposition (OCP), 76
Output indicators, 92–94

P&G, 19
Personal alignment, 95–98
Personal feedback, 39
Personal Value Profiler (PVP), 75–76, 96
Personal values, 96
  example ranking of, 77
  one team, one vision, one mission, 77
  values as extensions of, 75–77
Personalised coaching, 98
Pfizer, 19
PI consultants, 69
PIOL, 69
  consulting company, 84
Post-deal management, 35
Post-merger, 24
Pre-deal management, 35
Pre-merger, 24
Project planning, 28
Protectionism, 9
Purpose, 89
  approaches to discovering key purpose, 57
  assessment, 56
  culture and values, 57–59
  finding purpose, 56–57
  M&A software diagnostic scan, 59–61
  realizing business benefits of merger/acquisition, 65–66
  tensions revealed by our OCP, 61–65

PWC research, 23
PWCC, 55

Readers, 18, 59
Realising benefits
  systemic alignment, 95–98
  value and culture awareness programmes, 99–100
Recent crises, 7
Regional government, 4
Regulatory approvals, 17
Regulatory interventions, 17
Rigorous approach, 29
Risk measures, 21
Rooting benefits
  systemic alignment, 95–98
  value and culture awareness programmes, 99–100

Savings evaluation, 27–28
Self-confidence, 42
Semiconductors, 9
Shared value, 81
Shareholder value, 32, 35, 69, 89
  in M&A process, 12
Shareholders, 1
Simplistic approach, 65
Skepticism, 7
Sledge hammer, 12
Small enterprises, 102
Small family businesses, 102
Smartphone, 103
Société Suisse pour l'Industrie Horlogère (SSIH), 2
Soft issues, 28
  due diligence, 28
  failure to communicate effectively, 30–31
  failure to elicit and focus on key issues, 27
  failure to question (cultural) assumptions, 28–29
  integration project planning, 28
  interim conclusions concerning M&A failures, 31–32

Index

merger goals, 32–33
resolving cultural issues, 29–30
selecting management team, 29
synergy and savings evaluation, 27–28
SpaceX, 44
Stakeholders, 1
   relationship management processes, 35
Starbucks, 4
Strategic alliances, 4, 19
Strategic process, 38, 102
Structural alignment, 98
Structural process, 38, 102
Supplier process, 38, 102
Swiss watch industry, 2
Synergistic values, 35
Synergy
   evaluation, 27–28
   overestimation of, 15–16
Systematic approach, 29, 33
Systemic alignment, 95–96
   Group Alignment and Cohesion, 98
   personal alignment, 96–98
   structural alignment, 98
Systemic approach, 33
Systemic process, 38

Team, 77
   collects, 82
Technology sector, 9
Theory led professional practice, 101
Three phase framework
   creating (compelling) business case, 37
   developing implementation strategy, objectives, and key performance indicator, 39
   developing systemic alignment and value awareness, 39–40
   step by step in, 37
   step wise activities for phase A, 39
   step wise activities for phase B, 40
   step wise activities for phase C, 40
Three-phase process, 102
Top-down process, 42
Total value, 19
Triangulated approach, 29
Trompenaars Hampden-Turner (THT), 103

Unexpected costs, 15
'Unicorn' culture, 53–54
UniCredit, 67, 69
US Guided Missile Culture, 94

Value to behaviours (V2B), 70, 81–84, 89
   example four part charter, 82–83
Value(s), 57–58, 67, 79
   alignment, 98
   approaches to discovering key purpose, 57
   assessment, 56
   awareness programmes, 99–100
   conceiving values as integral verbs, 69–75
   of core values, 67–69
   culture and values, 57–59
   dilemmas, 66
   exploring core values of organisation by metaphors, 77–80
   as extensions of personal values, 75–77
   finding purpose, 56–57
   as giving life to purpose and mission, 75
   intact teams, 84
   levels, 89
   M&A software diagnostic scan, 59–61
   measurements, 58–59
   organisation of core values, 80
   orientations, 51, 73
   realizing business benefits of merger/acquisition, 65–66

selecting values, 66–67
tensions revealed by our OCP, 61–65
translating V2B, 81–84
translating values into (effective) behaviours, 81
Vision, 31, 77, 89
  redefining, 41–44

Wal-Mart, 43
WebApps, 103
Well-developed processes, 59
Western technology, 9
Whole system integration process, 85
Wide talent programme, 71

www.ingramcontent.com/pod-product-compliance
Lightning Source LLC
Jackson TN
JSHW081944240825
89903JS00004B/8